Kissing in Columbus

*Romantic things to see and do
in and around Ohio's capital*

Amber Stephens and
Jennifer Poleon

**Emuses
Columbus, Ohio**

Published by Three Muses Co., LLC d/b/a Emuses
P.O. Box 1264
Worthington, OH 43085-1264

Credits
Book design: Kathy Murphy
Edited by: Robin Smith
Front Cover photograph: Randall L. Schieber

On the cover
Front cover, The Topiary Garden at Old Deaf School Park, E. Town St. and Washington Ave., Columbus. Back cover, patio dining at the Inn at Cedar Falls, photo courtesy of the Inn at Cedar Falls.

The publisher and authors have done their best to ensure the accuracy of information in *Kissing in Columbus*. Prices, phone numbers etc. were correct as of press time. However, it's always smart to call and confirm information before heading out. The publisher assumes no responsibility for any loss, injury or inconvenience sustained by visitors as a result of information obtained or advice provided by this book.

ISBN 0-9723153-2-2

5 4 3 2 1

Contents

The simplest of romantic possibilities, and perhaps the most underrated. Who could resist the crunch of autumn leaves, the heady aromas of a sun-warmed herb garden, or the crisp snap of a just-picked apple? Or for the urban-minded, perhaps a Victorian neighborhood stroll or jazz in the park? Pick a spot and step into the slow lane with your special someone.

Dinner out—the classic date. But classic doesn't have to mean the same old, same old. Try a Greek dinner complete with belly dancers, or maybe Cuban and kitsch (ever wonder what became of that spiky '60s clock from your grandmother's living room?) Choose cuisine from fine to funky; after all, variety is the spice of love.

Ah, sweet seduction. Sometimes that little something special is the difference between "I had a nice time" and—well, we'll leave it to your imagination. Top off an autumn walk with a fabulously rich cream puff. Follow up the theater with latte and creamy raspberry cheesecake. Or cuddle up with Casablanca *and a sinfully smooth bowl of ice cream and two spoons. Mmm.*

Admit it, sometimes dinner out is just too much to deal with. For nights when you and your sweetie just want to kick back and relax, may we suggest fine wines and a tapas sampler? A martini and some smooth jazz? Perhaps a locally brewed ale and a game of darts, or even hot Chinese tea and a long talk? Playing footsie is optional but highly recommended.

Stuck on the dinner-and-movie treadmill? Turn up the flames of love and learn to tango instead. Take in some cabaret, rock-n-roll style. Thrill to music under the stars. The possibilities are endless, and we have the suggestions to prove it. Skip the meal and megaplex this week and rev up the romance!

Romantic Outings by Interest

Acknowledgements

The authors and publisher would like to gratefully acknowledge the enthusiasm we received from all the people in and around Columbus as we put this book together. Thanks for your suggestions. Thanks for your time. Thanks for your support. Thanks to Bill and Samuel for being great "dates." And thanks as always to Robin and Kathy. You make things run.

For our loved ones and those who have provided inspiration over the years.

Kissing in Columbus

Have you ever wished you knew of something new and different to do with your significant other? A quiet place to just walk and hold hands? Someplace to spend Saturday night other than the same old movie and the same old restaurant?

Now there's help for the date-challenged in central Ohio: Kissing in Columbus, *a compendium of romantic places and ideas for dates and days to remember. Find out where you can take a romantic hot-air balloon ride for two; watch belly dancers over dinner; stroll through a fragrant herb garden; spend a summer weekend in a gypsy wagon; or do just drinks and a jazz combo.*

As longtime and lifelong residents of central Ohio, we knew the area had some romantic gems just waiting to be discovered. What we weren't expecting was a whole mine of them! From moonlit canoe rides to smooth jazz in a cozy nightclub, the Columbus area has something new lovers, married couples, dating professionals and everyone in between can enjoy.

While there are so many topics that could be covered for Kissing in Columbus, *we tried to narrow it down to a few our readers would find interesting, inventive or unique. For example, with the area's large student population, thanks to The Ohio State University, Otterbein College and other higher learning institutions, it just made sense to include a chapter called Cheap Dates. After all, the time when many young adults do the most dating is when wallets are also the thinnest.*

Some topics, such as Food of Love, are so extensive that they could have been a book unto themselves. Columbus is home to thousands of restaurants and we clearly could not cover them all. But we could highlight the venerable institutions, such as The Refectory, or talk about where you can be transported to exotic locales. With new restaurants springing up daily, and some of them fading just as quickly, we decided to cover establishments that had proven their worth and would most likely still be open when you set out for your romantic dinner.

Of course not all dates have to be set over dinner and a movie. With an open mind, and perhaps some athletic ability, an Adventure Date could be just as much fun. For a quieter low-key date, try one of the ideas in Great Places to Walk and Hold Hands. If you are looking for other nontraditional ideas, check Beyond Dinner and a Movie and learn where you can tango or even listen to a Frank Sinatra impersonator.

Of course there's more to a romantic outing than dinners out, slow walks, and dancing 'til dawn. Sometimes dating means gift giving or romantic weekend sleepovers. From a Scottish getaway to a chocolate fantasy hotel package, central Ohio has great places to linger and get caught kissing.

So whether you are a new couple in love or a married couple just looking to find a few hours alone, Kissing in Columbus *is sure to provide you with new ideas to spark the flame or relight the torch.*

Places to Kiss:
Ideas to Get You Started

Pecking on the Patio
Enjoy an early tapas dinner (preferably on the patio), followed by a stroll through tree-lined brick streets (pg. 32).

Kiss, Movie-star Style
Pretend you're Fred Astaire and Ginger Rogers (or learn to) during a Friday-night dance party (pg. 54); spend those hot summer Saturdays in balcony seats watching classic movies starring the likes of Cary Grant and Grace Kelly (pgs. 100 and 106); or rent out a whole theater and show your favorite romantic film (pg. 58).

Go French
Spend the day picnicking along the banks of the "Seine" (pg. 93) or holding hands at a Paris-style outdoor cafe (pg. 31).

Kiss Like It's New Year's Eve
Try dinner at a swanky downtown restaurant accompanied by a New Year's Eve style champagne toast (pg. 49). Then stay in one of Columbus' most comfortable beds. Arrange for late check-out and a couple's massage. (pg. 80)

I Can't Believe You Can Do This in Columbus

- Hike to our own waterfall, located just minutes from downtown
- Picnic in a park featuring a famous Impressionist painting come to life
- Go sailing
- Take a canoe ride accompanied by tiki torches and Italian opera
- Attend premiere movies
- Indulge in high English tea

Feel like a Kid Again
Experience young love again: ride a carousel (pgs. 20 and 84), play Skeeball (pg. 57), or bowl through the wee hours, then go for breakfast. (pg. 99).

Worthy of a Prince and Princess
Climb a tower gazebo and proclaim love for your paramour (pg. 20) or spend the night in a castle (pgs. 85–86).

Love and Politics in the Afternoon
Listen to a midday lecture on the issues of the day, then steal a lunchtime smooch (pg. 76).

One Hot Date
Share an appetizer of flaming cheese (pg. 30); get cozy by the fireplace sipping wine on a couch or in a French bistro (pgs. 47 and 31); or opt for a couple's hot stone massage (pg. 80).

Picnics with Pop
Pack the wine and cheese and your favorite blanket for a picnic starring Shakespeare (pgs. 18 and 105); the symphony (pg. 57); local jazz bands (pgs. 18 and 106); or a favorite author (pg. 74).

Great PLACES
to WALK
& HOLD HANDS

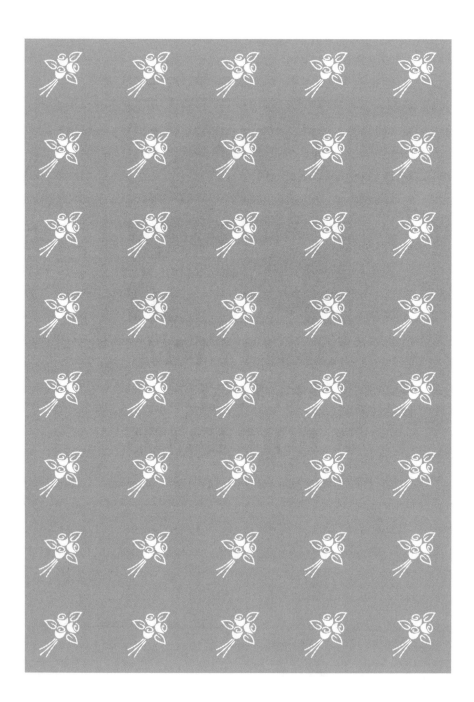

The crunch of leaves underfoot, the feel of your lover's hand enveloped in your own and the cadence of footsteps completely in sync all make for a memorable outdoor walk. Some walkers enjoy the bustle of a busy park or the ease of walking in an open field, while others prefer the serene setting of a riverside ramble or the challenges of a strenuous hillside hike. You'll find ideas that cross all seasons...the new bloom of flowering trees in the spring, the full-blown roses of summer, the mysterious mazes of fall and the heartwarming, mittens-required, lighted holiday stroll. Give yourself all day or an extended afternoon to breathe in nature and reacquaint your senses with central Ohio's outdoor offerings. Even in the city, nature is just waiting for us to follow. And regardless of season or location, the activity that is good for our romancing hearts is also good for our beating hearts. With a little ingenuity you can find that perfect path to claim as your favorite route. Your heart will thank you for it.

Grand Old Parks

Created before the turn of the 20th century, **Goodale Park** in Victorian Village and **Schiller Park** in German Village are two of the city's oldest and most beloved retreats. As the oldest park in the city, Goodale is also blessed with some of the grandest trees. This 32-acre nature escape welcomes lovers with its inviting landscape, historic park shelter and romantic gazebo. Jazz fills the air on summer Sunday afternoons, while canine friends fill the park each evening for a local meet and greet. *120 W. Goodale Blvd., www.columbusrecparks.com.*

The setting is just as serene at Schiller Park in the center of German Village. Sing in the rain à la Gene Kelly near the park's Umbrella Girl statue or recite quotations to each other from the park's namesake German poet (his words can be found inscribed in granite along the brick promenade). Schiller Park offers its own summer treat: free Shakespeare in the Park courtesy of Actors' Theatre. Bring a blanket and enjoy the Bard after a stroll through Schiller. *Located between Jaeger Street, City Park, Reinhard and Deshler Avenues, www.germanvillage.org/schillerpark.htm or www.columbusrecparks.com.*

Secret Garden in the Suburbs

Westerville's **Inniswood Metro Gardens**, the jewel of the Columbus Metro Parks, is a tranquil 123-acre nature retreat that's more arboretum than outdoor amusement area. Here walkers can smell the flowers spilling along paved walkways or take the boardwalk trail into the woods without worrying about in-line skaters, joggers or other "active sports," which are prohibited on the walking trails. Lovers can spend quiet moments walking in the park's Rock Garden next to the Innis House where a babbling stream flows among the well-tended flora. Or sit and enjoy the scene from one of the benches. If this setting isn't romantic enough, try a walk through the herb garden, which features its own Bible garden and beautiful vine-covered gazebos, perfect for a quick garden kiss. If all the romantic settings have made you feel like a kid again, go to the Sisters' Garden for a turn through the Story

Maze. With more than 2,000 species of plants and a variety of specialty collections, Inniswood's atmosphere is as changing and beautiful as the seasons. Although this is a romantic place to walk hand-in-hand or talk peacefully on a bench, it's not a place to picnic. That's prohibited for two-legged creatures. *940 S. Hempstead Rd., Westerville, 614-895-6216, www.metroparks.net.*

Scholarly Strolls

For many young adults, campuses are as much about coupling as cramming. On Ohio State University's famous **Oval**, lovers who take The Long Walk from the east end of the Oval to the west end, where a statue of William Oxley Thompson stands guard in front of the library, are destined for matrimony. If you're not ready to make that much of a commitment, even in theory, the Oval is still a great place to take a walk, watch dogs playing catch or even hang out for some studying in the sun. **Just off College Avenue on OSU's campus, Columbus.**

Ohio State isn't alone in its walking superstitions, though. Over at Capital University, legend says that couples who walk through the wrought-iron gates on the Main Street entrance are also headed to the altar. But don't leave campus with your sweetheart under those same gates before you graduate. That means you'll be leaving without a diploma! **Capital entrance gate, off Main Street, on Capital University's campus, Bexley.**

Stop and Smell the Roses

If you've ever promised your love a world of roses and sunshine, then take a stroll through the **Park of Roses**. With more than 11,000 rose bushes of some 350 varieties from miniature to climbing, the park is an olfactory delight. Summer is high season for seeing and smelling all of the bursting buds, but spring has its offerings too, with a lush daffodil garden. Climb the wrought iron tower gazebo for a full view of all the park's glory. It's a great spot for a relaxing view of the roses. You might even glimpse an outdoor wedding or hear a summer concert coming from the gazebo. A perennial garden and herb garden round out the park's botanical offerings. Adjacent to the park is the massive **Whetstone Park**, featuring ball fields, a fishing pond and miles of walkways. *3923 N. High St., Columbus.*

Walk with the Animals

Dorothy was scared to walk with the lions and tigers and bears, oh, my!, but the **Columbus Zoo and Aquarium** has all the offerings of a romantic hand-in-hand walk. With eight habitat areas, including the African Forest and Islands of Southeast Asia, the zoo has it all, from the gorgeous landscaping and easily navigated walkways to all of the beautiful animals. Where else in town can you cross over a Balinese bridge and enter a world of Asian small-clawed otters and orangutans? Or enjoy petting gentle goats followed by watching prairie dogs scurrying in and out of their dens? You can even ride the lavishly restored carousel together. And of course there are plenty of vendors just waiting to sell you a cool ice cream treat on a hot summer day.

But as fun as a trip to the zoo can be in the summer, the zoo's annual winter Wildlights show is just as spectacular. Buy a cup of steaming cocoa to keep you warm while viewing the city's ultimate outdoor holiday display with more than 2 million lights. You might even want to try a hand-in-hand outdoor ice skate. It's a winter wonderland for children, adults and the animals. *9990 Riverside Dr., Powell, 614-645-3550, www.colszoo.org.*

Into the Woods

Hand holding is a nice gesture on most walks, but during a trail trek in one of central Ohio's Metro Parks, it just might be required. With steep terrain and slippery slopes, some of the park system's trails are not for the light hearted. But don't despair! There are 14 parks in the system, many of them featuring trails that are pedestrian friendly, such as **Heritage Trail's** 3.3 mile ADA accessible multipurpose trail. And for those who seek a challenge, there are trails that feature hilly landscapes, such as **Chestnut Ridge's** 1-mile **Ridge Trail**. This trail even has a reward: an observation deck where lovers can linger and enjoy a view of the surrounding hills and forests or the Columbus skyline off in the distance. No matter how long you've lived in Columbus, there is likely to be at least one park you haven't visited, including one of the newer additions, **Glacier Ridge** or **Three Creeks**. The parks are all different, but they all have well-maintained facilities and beautiful walking trails, hand holding optional. *Main offices, 1069 W. Main St., Westerville, 614-508-8000, www.metroparks.net.*

Fall for Each Other

The corn is high, the path is unmarked, and your map is back at the car. With just the two of you to make it through one of the area's corn mazes, this could take a while. But hey, it's one of the few times most of us have the chance to be surrounded by a curtain of corn. The six-acre corn maze at **Circle S Farm** near Grove City might not have an elaborate crop circle formation, but it can be intimidating nonetheless. For a twist on the tradition, also try the farm's sunflower maze. Top off the trailblazing with a pumpkin donut from their Pickin' Patch Bakery before heading out on the wagon to find your own pumpkin in the large fields. *9015 London Groveport Rd., Grove City, 614-878-7980, www.circlesfarm.com.* At **Lynd Fruit Farm** on the opposite side of town, you can also lose yourselves in two miles of corn pathways, if you're not already getting lost in the orchards (see As Good As Apple Pie, pg. 22). Each year the farm's corn crew develops a new and elaborate corn maze. For an extra challenge, try it together in the dark during October weekends. *Corner of St. Rte. 310 and Morse Rd., Pataskala, 740-927-1333, www.lyndfruitfarm.com.*

As Good as Apple Pie

Maybe it's the fall weather or the beautiful colors of autumn, but whatever the reason, walking together in just the right orchard setting can be as romantic as strolling along the beach. And locals know that during September and October **Lynd Fruit Farm** is the place to grab an empty bag (10 pound or 20 pound capacity) and hit the rows. Tempt your lover with one of the local homegrown varieties of apple, such as Winesap, Melrose, Goldrush or Red Delicious. Together you can shoulder the load while choosing the perfect apples with just the right blush and crispness. Thankfully the trees are just short enough that you don't have to shoulder each other while trying to pick. Back at home, bake an apple pie together to enjoy outside in the cool autumn air. It's a sweet temptation for any couple. *Corner of St. Rte. 310 and Morse Rd., Pataskala, 740-927-1333, www.lyndfruitfarm.com.*

Homes, Sweet Homes

There are plenty of great places to walk and hold hands in just about any neighborhood. Dublin is especially proud of its walking trails, and there are plenty of beautiful homes to gaze upon along the way. But why not dream of a home together while walking in the older neighborhoods of Bexley, Clintonville, German Village, Grandview or Worthington? The pedestrian pace is sure to reveal neighborhood beauties never noticed before.

History, Haunts and Hallowed Halls

Downtown and around town there are a plethora of architectural gems just waiting to tell their stories. And the **Columbus Landmarks Foundation** steps in to do just that with its annual walking tour series. From Capitol Square and the Brewery District to Old Beechwold and Rush Creek Village (the Frank Lloyd Wright-like neighborhood in Worthington), the walking tours present the area's history and architecture through a series of Wednesday, Saturday or Sunday walks held each summer and fall. Volunteers enlighten fellow walkers on everything from the area's history to architectural appointments. Other tours of interest include the annual self-guided City Hop downtown featuring newly renovated living spaces in historic buildings; the Halloween Ghost Walks, which visit some of Columbus' most famous haunts; and the Great Hallelujah Holiday Tour showcasing downtown's fabulous churches, complete with music. Because of the tours' popularity, advance ticket purchases are recommended. *61 Jefferson Ave., Columbus, 614-221-0227, www.columbuslandmarks.org.*

Reservoir Retreat

With Upper Arlington, Columbus and Dublin all within a stone's throw of **Griggs Reservoir**, this popular park is a close-to-home favorite for many local lovers. The park, on the east bank of the reservoir off Riverside Drive, has several entrance and exit locations, which can be

a little daunting for the first time visitor. We suggest parking at the lots near Fishinger Road and then exploring to your mutual hearts' content. Park-goers can enjoy fishing, boating, picnicking and cookouts. Or try the reservoir's disc golf course. And, of course, there are plenty of paved walking paths, more than seven miles altogether, for a calming walk along the water. Just be sure to watch for any motorists along the road-ways, which can also wind along the waterfront. There is plenty of action to watch on the water as well. Sailors, rowers, and fishers all partake of the reservoir's offerings. *2933 Riverside Dr., Columbus, www.columbusrecparks.com.* Be sure to check out nearby hidden **Hayden Falls**. Park in the lot on Hayden Run Rd. west of Riverside. The falls are down the hill and to the right. The trail is rocky; watch your step. Bring your sketch pad or camera!

Walking in a Wetland Wonderland

Just off the Olentangy River bikeway and the adjoining Whetstone Park rests a marshy haven for songbirds and waterfowl at the Ohio State University's **Olentangy River Wetland Research Park**. Walk in quiet tranquility to enjoy nature's song from croaking toads and honking geese to trilling red-winged blackbirds and chirping crickets. The wheelchair accessible **Sandefur Wetland Pavilion** is open daily to the public, providing an aerial view of the manmade wetlands, where you can marvel at "nature's kidneys" in action. Alert walkers might also come across a beaver, muskrat or red fox, so take along a camera for a close-to-home photo safari. *352 Dodridge St., Columbus, 614-247-7984, http://swamp.ag.ohio-state.edu/ORW.html.*

Cave Crawl

Southeast of Columbus, the **Hocking Hills** region is a deep-forested rock gorge and cliff retreat. There are six sections of the state park, each featuring natural beauty and plenty of opportunities for hiking. Visitors to **Ash Cave**, Ohio's largest recess cave, can leisurely walk along the wheelchair accessible path to view a 90-foot waterfall, while visitors to **Rock House**, the park's only truly cave-like formation, have a more arduous trek up hill-hugging trails. And no trip to the region would be complete without visiting the granddaddy of the park: **Old Man's Cave**, with its gorges, devil's bathtub and whispering falls. This region is usually the busiest, even featuring a snack stand in the summertime, so check into other areas for a more tranquil ramble. Other notable stops include **Cantwell Cliffs** and **Cedar Falls**. And there are other parks and

preserves along the way that are not part of the state park system but offer great hikes nonetheless, including **Clear Creek Metro Park**, **Rockbridge State Nature Preserve** or Ohio Historical Society's **Wahkeena Preserve**, named for the Indian word for "most beautiful." With Wahkeena's sandstone cliffs, pond,

Hocking Hills in the spring

orchids, rhododendrons and 69 species of birds, it is indeed! If you are going for an all-weekend outing, check out the **Inn at Cedar Falls**, **Glenlaurel** and **Ravenwood Castle** in our Romantic Getaways section. *Much of the region can be accessed off U.S. Rte. 33 along State Routes 664 and 374, Logan, 740-385-6841 (Park Office), www.hockinghillspark.com.*

Notes on Nature & Walking

In preparation for your walk through the woods or when the sunshine is in hibernation, there are any number of nature-themed books to stir our passions for the great outdoors. We've selected some of our favorites...good for sharing in front of a warm fire or even snuggled together on a picnic blanket.

Robert Frost: Seasons. With the gorgeous nature photography of Christopher Burkett, and the timeless words of Robert Frost, *Seasons* is an audio-visual escape to mother nature. Couples beginning a journey together, in life or just on the sidewalk, should especially read "The Road Not Taken." Of course, Frost's work can be found in dozens of books at any library and they all bring the feeling of nature home to readers.

Dream Work by Mary Oliver. In this collection of poems by Pulitzer-prize winning poet and Ohio native Mary Oliver, nature plays an integral role, as it does in most of Oliver's work. Her poems, often about life's journey, are lilting, joyful and perceptive, as evidenced by "Coming Home" and "At Sea."

Scratching the Woodchuck: Nature on an Amish Farm by David Kline. Kline's essays on nature, farming, animals and the seasons are written with the skill of a naturalist's eye and an essayist's turn of phrase to create an enthralling glimpse of Ohio's natural world. Topical chapters allow for reading in small spurts.

Walden by Henry David Thoreau. Of course you can't have even a short listing of nature books without noting the masterpiece of them all: *Walden*. If you're not moved to downsize, live in the woods, or at least go for a nature walk after reading Thoreau's timeless entries about life at Walden Pond in the 1840s, you need to start rereading from the beginning.

The Year of the Turtle by David M. Carroll. Artist and naturalist David Carroll follows a yearly cycle of freshwater turtles from springtime emergence to winter hibernation. His black and white illustrations capture the beauty of his words. One can't help thinking Carroll is a modern Thoreau.

WorldWalk by Steven Newman. Beginning in 1983, Steven Newman set out from Bethel, Ohio to become the first person to walk solo around the world. After 4 years and some 10,000 miles he accomplished his goal. This book recounts Newman's struggles and comforts along the way, with an upbeat world message.

FOOD
of LOVE

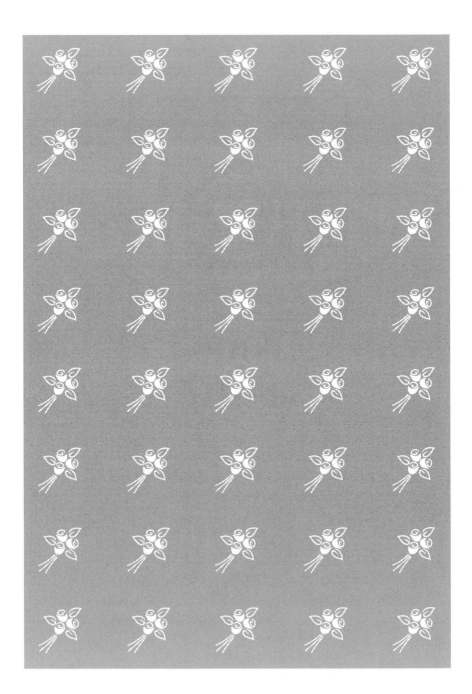

Dining is integral to dating, and particularly so here in central Ohio with all the great restaurant choices. Frankly we had a hard time choosing what places to include. Columbus has a plethora of eateries known for their great food and great settings, but we wanted to look beyond just the most well-known date-night choices. We finally decided that the majority of the restaurants should be heavy on romantic ambiance and have a proven reputation. (Although great new restaurants open everyday, we chose to highlight those that have been serving a while.) Even so, there are many noteworthy restaurants for date making that, while lacking interior refinement, still offer up a great meal to share with your best gal or guy. We've even included suggestions for vegetarian and vegan-friendly restaurants. So instead of ending up at the same handful of restaurants on your precious nights out, or simply going to the most expensive restaurants around because they are supposed to be good, shake it up and keep your dates like your food—fresh!

Dining Around the World

Columbus benefits from the world influence of major corporations and OSU's large foreign student population, as well as many foreign-born citizens who call Columbus home. Most people would never guess that our capital boasts restaurants ranging from Indian, Vietnamese, Japanese, and Ethiopian fare to fine Latin American, Greek, Italian and European-inspired cuisines. With so many to choose from, you can take a tour of the world for weeks on end.

That's Amoré

Imagine your ideal romantic Italian restaurant and you have **Trattoria Roma** in Grandview. It's part pure Italy and part the American interpretation of such. Couples are serenaded with music by Dean Martin, Frank Sinatra and Ella Fitzgerald while they dine at cozy candlelit tables for two topped with small Pellegrino water bottle vases. The food is decadent, starting with appetizers such as the Gorgonzola mushroom polenta or entrees featuring interesting cream sauces. The wine list is strong and comes with several choices by the glass or half bottle. For dessert try the pots de crème, a dense chocolate custard that is even richer than the best chocolate mousse. With some of the restaurant's great red wine and rich food in your belly and the songs of '50s crooners still ringing in your head, you're sure to leave primed for amoré. *1447 Grandview Ave., Columbus, 614-488-2104. Lunch. Dinner.*

Great Greek

You've got to like a place that has flaming cheese on the menu and belly dancers on the weekends. That's exactly what you'll find at **Taverna Opa**, the Greek restaurant that made the German Village dining scene even more interesting when it opened a few years ago. It's housed in a historic house that once was the home of an early Columbus mayor. During warmer months it has one of the nicer patios in town. The menu is big and includes several lamb creations from roast leg of lamb to lamb chops, among other traditional Greek fare, and of course, saganaki, the flaming cheese appetizer that's sure to heat up your date, that is, if the weekend belly dancers who sway from table to table don't do so first. *961 S. High St., Columbus, 614-444-0131. Lunch. Dinner.*

À la Paris

There are few restaurant destinations that could be more romantic than streetside Parisian cafés. Columbus doesn't have those, but we do have **La Chatelaine French Bakery and Café**, which does have outdoor seating at its two locations; however, we've found the downtown Worthington location to have much more of that intimacy and old-world charm than its sister location in Upper Arlington. If you are craving French breakfast omelettes, homemade French onion soup (what else?), wine or even beef bourguignon, La Chatelaine can feed your French habit three meals a day. Look for a seat near the fireplace. *1550 W. Lane Ave., Upper Arlington, 614-488-1911 and 627 N. High St., Worthington, 614-848-6711, www.lachatelainebakery.com. Breakfast. Lunch. Dinner.*

Sultan's Palace

Whisk your date away on a magic carpet ride to **Cafe Istanbul** at Easton. Let the romantic ambiance sweep you away to an exotic locale while you sample Turkish culinary delights. Experience a variety of dishes with the appetizer sampler, which comes with about a half dozen different options from hummus to grape leaves. (If you are braver than us, get the calf's liver appetizer!) Most dishes on the main menu are kabobs, but there are plenty of specialty items to choose from, including vegetarian dishes and seafood. Be sure to try the Turkish coffee as an appropriate cap to your meal. *3983 Worth Ave., Columbus, 614-473-9144, www.cafeistanbul.com. Lunch. Dinner.*

Sushi and Singing

There are plenty of other great Asian restaurants that have popped up in Columbus in recent years, but **Otani Restaurant and Sushi Bar** may still be the most fun. It is also one of the few that served sushi in Columbus long before it became popular in the Midwest. After a few thimbles of saki on Friday and Saturday evenings, you can impress your date with your best *American Idol* performance during the restaurant's Karaoke night. The restaurant specializes in, not surprisingly, great sushi choices and tempura. The low tables and kimono-wearing waitresses help make this an authentic Japanese-inspired experience. *Off 161 and I-71, 5900 Roche Dr., Columbus, 614-431-3333. Lunch. Dinner.*

Swanky & Special

The Art of Italian

Rigsby's Kitchen is everything a big city restaurant should be. It's also everything a date restaurant should be, with chic décor, a strong wine list, and live music several nights a week. If the ambiance and artwork aren't enough to keep your eyes satisfied, behind the large marble counter you can check out the chefs preparing signature Northern Italian dishes such as the penne arrabiata or parsley roasted halibut. Rigsby's is also a great place to see and be seen during the Short North's monthly Gallery Hop. Just make sure to reserve a table well in advance. *698 N. High St., Columbus, 614-461-7888. www.rigsbyskitchen.com. Closed Sundays. Valet Parking. Lunch. Dinner.*

Tapas for Two

The warmth of wood and fine detailing marry beautifully with the cool modern lighting and wrought iron touches at **Barcelona** in the heart of German Village. Once home to accordion music and Saturday-night sing-alongs, this former neighborhood bar is now a trendy restaurant where daters can share a combination of tapas plates or indulge in a dinner plate all their own. For those who prefer a bit of both, try the large Barcelona Tapas Platter with a selection of items from roasted roma tomatoes to spiced olives. And while it isn't always on the menu, we suggest ordering the key lime martini. It's like dessert in a glass. During warmer months, ask for a seat on the patio. *263 E. Whittier St., Columbus, 614-443-3699, www.barcelonacolumbus.com. Valet Parking. Lunch. Dinner.*

Cozy and Classic

Don't let the unassuming exterior of the Bexley Square complex fool you into thinking that **Bexley Monk Restaurant and Bar** is just another run-of-the-mill dining establishment. For more than 20 years, patrons have been welcomed into this warm and inviting restaurant with live music nearly every night of the week. Cozy up together inside one of the Monk's wooden booths or just enjoy some drinks together at the bar. With a range of menu options from stone oven Margherita pizza to rack of lamb, there is something to appease a range of appetites. This is also one place that doesn't skimp on the quality of its side dishes. *2232 E. Main St., Bexley, 614-239-6665, www.bexleysmonk.com. Lunch. Dinner.*

Feast on Fine French Cuisine

When it comes to naming one of Columbus' most renowned restaurants, **The Refectory** inevitably makes everyone's short list. With its quiet dining nooks complete with candle-lit settings inside a renovated 19th-century church and schoolhouse, The Refectory has cornered the market on romantic ambiance. The menu changes frequently, but it is most decidedly rich French cuisine from the duck to the mousse. The award-winning wine list is also not to be missed. If the main dinner menu is a bit out of budget, ask for the lower-priced three-course bistro menu served in the lounge area Monday-Thursday. Then again, if you're going to sup at romance's finest table, it's probably best to bring the extra dough and splurge. *1092 Bethel Rd., Columbus, 614-451-9774, www.refectory.com. Dinner.*

Dine with the Master

It's hard to go wrong at **Handke's Cuisine**, owned by Columbus' most well-known chef, Hartmut Handke. The German restaurateur is one of a handful of chefs nationwide to be a Certified Master Chef, not to mention the fact that Handke is the first American to ever win a gold medal in the Bocuse d'Or international food competition. So you know you are in good hands here. This is the kind of place where extra food just appears at your table, interesting amuse bouches that delight the tongue. As for atmosphere, the restaurant oozes intimacy with its curved coves and gently glowing lighting, all within the confines of a 19th-century Bavarian brewery. Like other swank dining establishments, the eclectic menu changes throughout the year, but it's always fine cuisine. *520 S. Front St., Columbus, 614-621-2500, www.chefhandke.com. Closed Sundays. Valet Parking. Dinner.*

A Seaside Scene

If you are planning an evening of art appreciation during the Gallery Hop or even a night of hockey in the Arena District, stop in at **RJ Snapper's** for a romantic send-off to your date. With its mock Italian fishing village streetscape, with strings of white lights you'll feel transported from the streets of the Short North to the seascape of a European café. The menu focuses primarily on seafood, with traditional seafood specialties such as crab cakes and lobster and a variety of "Snapper's fresh fish with imagination" dishes that include creations such as the sake marinated Chilean sea bass. However, even landlubbers can find a steak or veggie plate on the menu. *700 N. High St., Columbus, 614-280-1070, rjsnappers.com. Valet Parking. Dinner.*

Top Patios

For those who like to dine al fresco, there is a large selection of patios around town. Here are a few of our favorites.

- **G. Michael's in German Village,**
  595 S. Third St., Columbus, 614-464-0575.
- **La Chatelaine, Worthington location**
  (see listing, pg. 31).
- **Haiku Poetic Food and Art in the Short North,**
  800 N. High St., Columbus, 614-294-8168.
- **Seven Stars at the Worthington Inn,**
  649 High St., Worthington, 614-885-2600.
- **Trattoria Roma**
  (see listing, pg. 30).
- **Barcelona in German Village**
  (see listing, pg. 32).

Fun and Funky

Bow Wow Bistro

Any restaurant named after the owner's poodle fits our bill as a fun place. But **Lulu's** has more than a fun name to set your tail waggin'. The fare is American comfort food, with a pleasantly upscale twist. The Eastern shore crab cakes, Tuscan-style ravioli, and fried green tomatoes are a sure bet, and the "Poodle Chicken," a cheese stuffed chicken breast wrapped in a pastry crust, is also a favorite. Then again, so is the décor, which includes everything from live goldfish swimming in bowls on the table to leopard-print carpeting on the floors. *1788 W. Fifth St., Columbus, 614-485-0559, www.luluscolumbus.com. Closed Sundays. Dinner.*

Flash from the Past

The '50s kitsch at the **Starliner Diner**, such as starburst wall clocks, and the colorful interior from the aqua blue booths to the large sun and moon mural, definitely let you know that you've entered the epicenter of fun and funky dining. This Hilliard landmark is known for its Southwestern, Mexican, and Cuban influenced dishes, including everything from huevos rancheros to cajun jambalaya. The plantain appetizer with yogurt dipping sauce is still one of the best things on the menu. And the handwritten menu board has some of the best specials in town. For those with an American palate, there are plenty of sandwiches and pizza options. *5420 Cemetery Rd., Hilliard, 614-529-1198, www.starlinerdiner.com. Closed Mondays. Breakfast. Lunch. Dinner. On Sunday Brunch only.*

Designer Pizza Pie

Want to try something special, but don't want to break the bank on unfamiliar gourmet cuisine? Then take your date out for pizza! Not pizza from a cardboard box, but pizza from the wood-fired ovens at **Spagio**. These designer pizzas offer a range of specialty items from smoked duck to spicy shrimp. The pasta and other European and Pacific Rim dishes have been enjoyed at this eclectic Grandview location for more than 20 years.

We also recommend trying some of their fabulous desserts and people watching from the patio during decent weather. *1295 Grandview Ave., Columbus, 614-486-1114, www.spagio.com. Lunch. Dinner.*

Fondue for Two

The Melting Pot may build upon the fondue craze from the '70s, but the concept is based on actual Swiss cuisine. Take a hot pot, some beef juice, meat, vegetables, melted cheese, fruit, melted chocolate and a few "spears" for dipping and you have a meal at one of two Columbus area Melting Pot restaurants. It definitely makes for an interactive date. One caveat: Fondue may sound cheap, but it's not. The "Roman Feast" for two for example, which includes cheese fondue, salad, entrée, and chocolate dessert, will set you back more than $60. *Easton Location—4014 Townsfair Way, Columbus, 614-476-5500, and 5090 N. High St., Columbus, 614-846-7600, www.meltingpot.com. Dinner.*

Vegetarian Eats

In a city with nearly 1 million residents, you might expect quite a few vegetarian restaurants. Alas, that is not the case. Although most of our vegetarian restaurants sacrifice atmosphere and ambiance for wholesome food, they are still great places to go for a healthy night out on the town. Here are some of our favorite vegan, vegetarian, or vegetarian-friendly restaurants.

Storefront Spice and Everything Nice

Here at **Annapurna**, a very small vegetarian storefront restaurant at Columbus Square, the host and atmosphere are friendly and the foods are priced modestly, with most lunches or dinners around $6 (as of printing)! The foods, from the tasty samosa appetizer, a fried vegetable pocket filled with potatoes and green peas, to the mutter paneer, a pea based platter with a pleasant balance of sweet and spicy, are all vegetarian and Indian. If you're not familiar with Indian fare, just ask; they'll suggest some items for you. And, of course, you can try it all with a mango lassi or top it off with gulab jamun for dessert. *5657 Columbus Square, Columbus, 614-523-3640. Closed Mondays. Lunch. Dinner.*

A Bowl of Goodness
      While eating a bowl of **Benevolence Café's** hearty vegetarian
soups or a thick slice of their fresh baked breads, it's easy to imagine a
group of monks hovered over wooden tables, kneading that day's bread.
That's not the case here, but the food is so good you'll want to give thanks.
The soup and bread menu changes daily, but there are enough varieties to
suit just about any taster's preference, from red potato and green bean soup
to tomato carrot bisque. If you're not in the mood for soup or salad, try a
sandwich from the à la carte menu, such as the hummus salad sandwich
or good ole peanut butter and jelly. The seating is communal and the
atmosphere is one of wholeness. For those who prefer to be more at one
with just your date, grab a pint of soup to go in a returnable Mason jar.
41 W. Swan St., Columbus, 614-221-9330, www.benevolencecafe.com.
Closed Sundays. Breakfast Saturday. Lunch. Dinner.

Vegan Phoenix
      In the best-of-the-best restaurant reviews around Columbus,
Dragonfly neo-v always makes the top 10 lists, whether it's a review of
vegetarian restaurants or the swankest joints in town. And we couldn't
agree more. With its artsy, modern décor, in the home of the former
King Avenue Coffee House, Dragonfly is the phoenix rising from the
ashes of a former vegetarian hotspot. The vegan menu features locally
grown produce to create such dishes as the delicious sun-dried tomato
risotto and the flavorful wild walnut ricotta ravioli. Enjoy a cup of green
tea with dinner or one of the restaurant's whimsically named drinks,
such as blood, a combination of celery, apple, beet and echinacea. The
menu changes seasonally and dinner specials are offered nightly. This is
by far Columbus' most upscale vegetarian restaurant and the best one
for a truly intimate, special vegan date. *247 King Ave., Columbus,*
614-298-9986, www.dragonflyneov.com. Closed Sundays and Mondays.
Saturday Brunch. Dinner.

One Scorching Café

Just west of Annapurna in the Village Centre is another pure vegetarian Indian eatery known as **Udipi Café.** The café's understated interior doesn't call attention to itself, but the food certainly does. The long paper-thin crepes (dosai) stuffed with a variety of options from cream of wheat and rice to hot chutney can make just about any diner look like a conspicuous consumer. And if that doesn't draw attention to your plate, the batura, large plate-sized bread puffs, certainly will. Although the food is spicy southern Indian cuisine, there are items for the tender tongued, such as the masala dosai filled with potatoes and onions, or the yogurt and cucumber-based side sauce, raita. *2001 E. Dublin Granville Rd., Columbus, 614-885-7446. Closed Tuesdays. Lunch. Dinner.*

The Vegetarian Veteran

As Columbus' oldest vegetarian restaurant, **Whole World Restaurant and Bakery** has proven that it can stand the test of time and changing tastes. This cozy Clintonville restaurant with a light wood interior is a vegetarian's delight in close quarters. Diners can check the board in the back for daily specials ranging from soups such as cream of carrot and garbanzo tomato served with delicious toast points to the quiche or quesadilla of the day. The restaurant also offers a variety of meatless sandwiches, such as the crunchy cucumber sandwich and the well-known broccoli burger. For more mainstream cuisine, without the tofu and sprouts, try one of the pizzas, all of which come with the option of a whole-wheat crust. While your pizza bakes you can check out the eclectic antiques shop next door or peruse the dessert counter, with such yummies as coffee cookies and vegan granola bars. *3269 N. High St., Columbus, 614-268-5751. Lunch. Dinner.*

JUST
DESSERTS

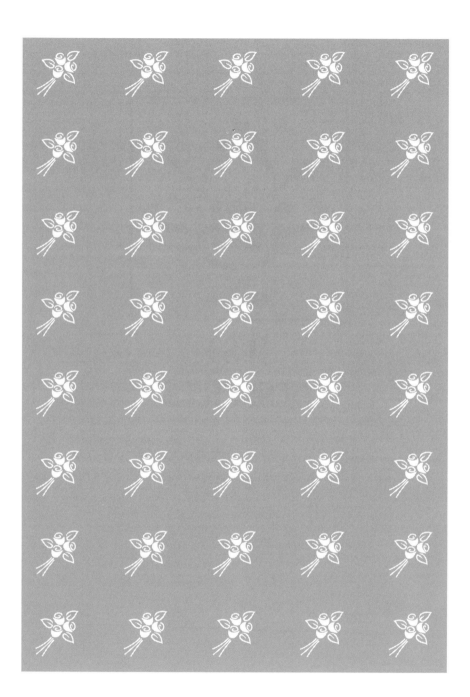

40

From two straws in a root beer float to two forks and a piece of pie, desserts are just made to be shared. You can get great dessert after dinner at many area restaurants, but why not make the dessert your destination? From Buckeye flavored ice cream to mango mousse cake, Columbus has an assortment of places made just for indulging. Some locations even offer "real" food, but why partake of the necessary when the luxuries are so much sweeter?

European Yum

A great place like German Village wouldn't be complete without an old-world-style bakery and dessert shop. Thankfully, **Juergen's Bakery and Restaurant** fills the void. Located in one of the traditional brick structures found throughout the village, Juergen's offers a plethora of Germanic desserts from cherry streusel-topped bars and scrumptious cream puffs to tempting cakes and cannolis. The "bee sting" dessert, which is as much of a mouthful to pronounce in German as it is to eat, is a creamy pastry dessert with a caramelized sugar and nut topping. Sit down and share a few desserts in the dining area and then walk it off with a stroll around the block or a short walk to Schiller Park. *525 S. Fourth St., Columbus, 614-224-6858. Closed Mondays.*

Coffees, Cakes and Comfort

The smell of hot java brewing is like a welcoming hug as soon as you enter a **Cup O' Joe**. And this is where central Ohioans come when they are ready to settle in with the laptop, research article, or newspaper. But that doesn't mean you can't drop in with your date after a movie at the Lennox or a shopping spree at Easton. Aside from the variety of espresso drinks, caffe lattes, fruit smoothies, coffees, mocha freezes and just about any other type of caffeine-infused drink, is a showcase of fresh pastries and decadent desserts. Enjoy scones, muffins, rolls, cookies or a bagel or try one of the cakes, such as the white chocolate raspberry cheesecake that complements coffee perfectly. For something different, snuggle together on one of the comfy couches with some chai tea while eating vegan cookies prepared by a local bakery, but sold at the Joe. *Several central Ohio locations, including German Village, Lennox, Bexley, Clintonville, Easton, Pickerington and the Short North on the Cap at Union Station.*

Sorbet, So Good

There are so many things to love about the North Market, from the wide selection of interesting foods to the market experience itself.

But one thing that stands out, even at North Market, is **Jeni's Fresh Ice Creams**. Jeni's, which has been featured on the Food Network, is an ice cream stand with adults in mind. Flavors range from seasonal specialties such as fresh lemon and blueberries to one of Jeni's best sellers, Thai Chilli, a fantastic blend of coconut milk, peanut butter, toasted coconut and cayenne pepper. Other specialty items include sherbets and sorbets. During summertime, take your dip and your date to nearby Goodale Park for a cool treat in the shade. *59 Spruce St., Columbus, 614-228-9960, www.jenisicecreams.com.*

Double Dip Date

You scream for vanilla. Your date screams for butter pecan. And the kids scream for cookies and cream. What? OK, not all "dates" happen just between a couple. Sometimes you have to bring a couple of kids along. Whatever the combination, ice cream shops can be enjoyed by everyone, and everyone in central Ohio seems to agree that we all scream for **Graeter's**. With 11 central Ohio locations, they are sure to have a shop nearby. Feeling a little intimidated by all of the flavor options? Pick a parfait or a turtle sundae and enjoy it together. Or try one of the company's seasonal favorites such as apple cider sorbet. And if your date just happens to include children, enjoy your creamy dessert at the Bethel Road location, which not only includes a view of the ice cream making process, but also a separate play room for the kiddies. *2555 Bethel Rd., Columbus, 614-442-7622, www.graeters.com. Check Web site for additional central Ohio locations.*

Delightful Desserts

Tucked in the back of the Bethel Centre strip mall, **Golden Delight Bakery** offers everything a sweet tooth might crave from the bakery's signature fresh strawberry cake to their unusual seaweed cookies. The fluffy cream cakes with a pleasing, light icing include such flavors as green tea, mango mousse, mocha cappuccino, and peaches and cream. And there's a reason why Golden Delight touts its strawberry cake: it's a slice of dessert dreamery with fresh strawberries between double-layered white cake. If you're in the mood for something a little less dessert-like, the bakery also offers an assortment of steamed and small buns in a variety of flavors. The bakery's only drawback is its lack of seating (just one table) so you will probably want to grab some of their specialty treats for a nice after-dinner dessert at home. *1516 Bethel Rd., Columbus, 614-459-6888. Closed Mondays.*

One Fabulous Factory

The Cheesecake Factory may sound like an industrial dessert destination, but it's one of the sweetest spots at Easton, and it typically has the crowd to prove it. With more than 30 types of cheesecake, this is the destination for lovers of that rich and creamy dessert. But we're not talking plain-Jane cheesecake with cherries on top. These cakes take the best of the dessert world and whirl them into one scrumptious creation, such as the key lime cheesecake, Boston cream cheesecake or even Oreo cheesecake. There are other desserts on the menu (as well as a book of regular menu items), but we think it would be a shame to order carrot cake at a restaurant made for cheesecake. *3975 Townsfair Way, Columbus, 614-418-7600, www.thecheesecakefactory.com.*

Maestro's Mouth-Watering Muse

Mozart's Bakery and Piano Café in Clintonville has created a reputation as one of the area's finest places to sit and enjoy beautifully crafted and wonderful tasting desserts. See Cheap (& Romantic) Dates on pg. 92 for a complete listing. *2885 N. High St., Columbus, 614-268-3687, mozartscafe.com.*

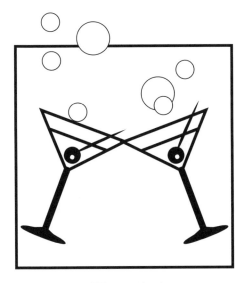

JUST
DRINKS

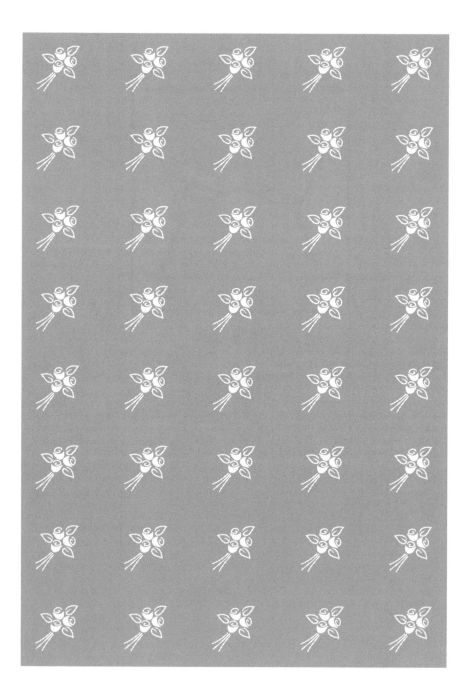

Some people may not want to admit it, but a lot of committed
couples met at a bar. For others, that's where romance started to blossom.
Sometimes date night starts too late for dinner out, and other times you
just want to meet, talk and chill out over something cool to drink.
(Or even a hot tea, for the teetotalers.) Just drinks doesn't have to
mean beer nuts and a Bud. You and your date can sample French wine
at a plush wine bar; have a cocktail at a jazz bar or perhaps a pint
at a pub; or sip on a martini in spots sure to make you feel Sex and
the City *cool.*

Wining and Dining

Columbus has a lot of happening bars and restaurants, but **The
Burgundy Room** may be the most romantic spot to meet up for a drink.
The hardwood floors and elegant interior in this wine bar will make the
two of you want to cozy up with a single bottle of wine at the bar or at
one of the tables made for people watching. Or take a wine "flight" and
sample several wines during the evening. The large tapas menu is a
perfect accompaniment to the wine selection and makes for a great way
to share a bite and a bottle. During the winter, head for a spot on the
leather couch near the fireplace at the Short North Arts District location.
641 N. High St., Columbus, 614-464-9463, or 6725 Avery-Muirfield Dr.,
Dublin, 614-798-9463, www.burgundyroom.net.

Capital City Cask

Columbus has a few microbreweries, but **Barley's Brewing Company Ale House No. 1** is the place to get the "perfect pint." From Barley's Pale Ale (its flagship brew) to varieties such as J. Scott Francis (the company's first cask conditioned brew), this is the place to taste Columbus' local froth. For those not inclined to beer, martinis and wine are also on the menu. For a little more privacy, ask to sit in one of the tall wooden booths. Or if you're feeling more social, try your hand at a game of darts. And oysters—those famous aphrodisiacs—are only $1 on Thursday! *467 N. High St., Columbus, 614-228-2537, www.barleysbrewing.com.*

Spirited and Fun

Betty's Fine Food and Spirits is a fun and kitschy, perhaps even cluttered, restaurant from the photos of '40s pinup girls and '50s print wallpaper to the knickknacks behind the bar. Even the food and drinks come with fun names, such as The Surly Girl Salad or the Betty Ford Clinic Special (pink lemonade and vodka). There are a variety of beers to be had at the bar, including locally made Columbus Brewing Pale Ale. The quarters are tight, which is a good reason (or excuse) to sit close. *680 N. High St., Columbus, 614-228-6191.*

Jazz It Up

Bexley Monk is a great restaurant in its own right; however, the attached bar hits just the right romantic note with jazz combo bands and intimate leather booths. Check the Web site for a listing of performers. See the listing in Food of Love on pg. 32 for complete details. *2232 E. Main St., Bexley, 614-239-6665, www.bexleysmonk.com.*

Overtime Opulence

Meeting for drinks downtown after work is just a few blocks away at **M** restaurant and bar, but it will make you feel a glamorous

world away from cubicles and fluorescent lights. At local restaurateur Cameron Mitchell's most upscale offering, revelers can enjoy mixed drinks, cocktails and other concoctions at the dramatically lit bar. The M champagne ice bar, complete with music, starts at 11 p.m. Friday and Saturday nights. Thursdays through Saturdays in the summer, enjoy your beverages outdoor on the patio with nightly music. *2 Miranova Place, Columbus, 614-629-0000, www.cameronmitchell.com. Valet Parking. Closed Sundays.*

Carrie & Mr. Big

Feel like you just stepped out of *Sex and the City* holding one of the specialty drinks at **Martini** in the Short North Arts District. Try one of the 18 martinis ranging from a chocolate martini to the traditional Cosmopolitan. A bit pricey, but worth the indulgence! Late Night@ Martini Short North starts Fridays and Saturdays at 10 p.m, featuring live music. If you're feeling like more than a nibble, the restaurant's Italian fare is some of the best around. For north enders, there's also a Martini off Polaris Parkway. *445 N. High St., Columbus, 614-224-8259. Valet Parking (evenings only). 1319 Polaris Pkwy, Columbus, 614-844-6500. www.cameronmitchell.com.*

Leaves in the Glass

Feel the Zen mood settle in at **ZenCha**, the sleek tea salon in the Short North. The salon offers a series of teas from a historic Chinese tea selection to a series of herbal remedy teas. If you don't know your teas, never fear, the staff will help you make a selection. All teas are served according to the region's custom. Try the bubble tea with tapioca for something really different. **982 N. High St., 614-421-2140, zen-cha.com.**

Have a Pint

So you want to take your favorite lass or lad to a British pub for a pint? Head to the original **Old Bag of Nails** in Olde Worthington for just the treat. It has all the trappings of an old-world bar, from a variety of brew to fish-n-chips. If the bar is crowded, as it can be in Worthington, grab a seat for two at a nearby table. If you're in the mood for a unique appetizer, try the beer-battered pickles. Or for a full meal, try one of their tasty burgers. *663 N. High St., Worthington, 614-436-5552, www.oldbagofnails.com. Check Web site for other local Old Bag of Nails locations.*

Wine Bar and More

Sit at red-checked covered bistro tables and indulge in any one of the **Spagio Cellars'** massive collection of wine bottles (for a cork fee). Having a hard time deciding? Then try a "taste" of a few types of wines. You can also pair your wine with cheese from their broad selection of international cheeses. They will even recommend which cheeses go with which wines. There are wine tastings each Thursday at 7 p.m., if you prefer to make just drinks a more formal affair. *1295 Grandview Ave., Columbus, 614-486-1114, www.spagio.com/cellars. Closed Mondays.*

Who Loves Ya, Baby?

Whenever **The Top Steak House** is mentioned, the '50s and the Rat Pack instantly spring to mind. This Columbus landmark, with its vintage charm, is most notably a steakhouse, but it's also a great place to relax at the bar. So if you are feeling like a time warp into old-Vegas style drinks (or dining), this is the establishment. Jazz performances add to the bygone-era feel. *2891 E. Main St., Columbus, 614-231-8238. Closed Sundays.*

Beyond DINNER
and a MOVIE

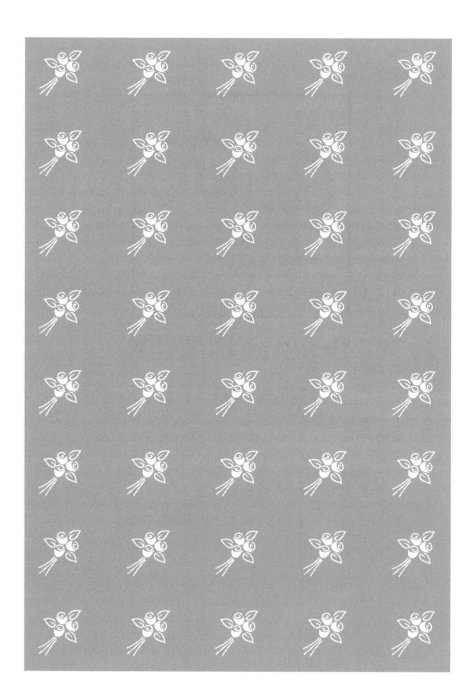

Dinner and a movie. It's the quintessential date. But through complacency, lack of creativity or courting rut, dinner and a movie often becomes boring and routine. Why settle for the super movie megaplex and a bucket of overpriced popcorn when there is so much more to do in Columbus?

To get you started out the door for a date night of something different, we've listed just a few of the many entertainment options waiting to be seized. There are arcade games and brewskies for the Xbox crowd or ballet along the riverbanks for the theatre-box crowd. We've even included a few multiple options for a single topic, such as three very different venues for enjoying jazz. And for those who can't quit clutching their movie tickets, we even have a selection of movie options that will let your companion know you put more thought into the date than just scanning the local listings. As they say over and over in one of our favorite movies, carpe diem!

Shall We Dance?

There's one at every wedding reception: the couple that tears up the dance floor while everybody else tries not to be embarrassed sashaying to the beat. With a few lessons and some Friday Night Parties, you can be that couple. For less than $50 you and your partner can take two introductory lessons at **Dance Plus**. The studio offers a variety of lesson options from private lessons to group lessons for couples, and even a pre-wedding crash course. Best of all, students (and outsiders) can practice their newly acquired skills every Friday night at a dance party, which features Big Band and Latino music. *1255 Grandview Ave., Columbus, 614-486-0471, www.dance-plus.com.*

Couples can also take up dance lessons and Friday Night Parties at Gahanna's **DanceCentre**, which was founded by Svetlana Iskhakov and her husband Igor. The couple met while dancing in Russia, and even took their waltz and tango moves to Japan to the World Dance Championships. The center offers a social dance and ballroom dance program as well as classes that kick up your heels a notch, such as hip hop, Argentine tango and belly dancing. *1000B Morrison Rd., Gahanna, 614-759-0502, www.columbusdancecenter.com.*

Music to Groove By

Your baby doesn't have to leave you for you to be in the mood for some good blues music. **Blues Station**, built to resemble a Southern juke joint with tin walls and open-air patio, is an Arena District hotspot. The crowd here can be mixed depending upon the night—part convention goer, part music lover. You can catch local blues acts or nationally known artists such as Tinsley Ellis. Along with live blues music Tuesday through Saturday, the Station also offers up a Southern menu of salads, sandwiches and BBQ. *147 W. Vine St., Columbus, 614-884-BLUE, www.bluesstation.net.*

Pirouettes with Your Paramour

For the uninitiated, the ballet can be intimidating. What if you don't understand it? What if your date doesn't like it? How long will it last? To get a taste for the ballet scene, each summer **BalletMet** performs a free show during Rhythm on the River downtown at Genoa Park (behind COSI). Performers in costume present a ballet sampler of the upcoming season in the Riverfront Amphitheater from the classic to the modern, with musical accompaniment. Once you see the preview, you'll be able to pick out the perfect performance for date night. Try the Met's annual *Nutcracker* performance. It's an awesome spectacle of dance and décor sure to put you in the holiday mood. Performances are held seasonally at the Ohio Theatre *(39 E. State St., Columbus)* and Capitol Theatre *(in the Riffe Center, 77 S. High St., Columbus). 614-229-4848 (box office), www.balletmet.org.*

From Smooth to Suave, a Jazz Triplet

After 40 years, **Dick's Den** is still serving up some of the best jazz in the city, in a nearly-perfect neighborhood bar atmosphere. Here you'll find cheap drinks, a pool table in the back and one of the best jukeboxes in town. You can 'lax out to the local jazz scene Thursday through Sunday. When the bands are not playing, throw some quarters in the jukebox to listen to Billie Holiday, Artie Shaw, Patsy Cline and more. *2417 N. High St., Columbus, 614-268-9573.*

Couples looking for jazz in a more refined setting will appreciate the bar at the **Bexley Monk Restaurant and Bar**. Intimate booths, a great wrap-around bar, and jazz six nights a week make for a swank evening of jazz. See Food of Love on pg. 32 for a complete listing. *2232 E. Main St., Bexley, 614-239-6665, www.bexleysmonk.com.*

If you want to go all out for an evening of music with the jazz masters, the **Columbus Jazz Orchestra** frequently brings in top jazz acts such as Branford Marsalis to the restored Southern Theatre. Be sure to check out CJO's own concerts offering swing, big band and classical jazz. With the largest subscription base of any jazz series in the United States, the CJO has proven itself to be all that jazz. *939 N. High St., Columbus, 614-294-5200, www.columbusjazzorchestra.com.*

Come Fly Away with Frank

Does your better half love Old Blue Eyes? Are you swayed into romance by the everlasting charm of "Come Fly with Me," "I Get a Kick Out of You," or "My Funny Valentine?" If so, good news! Michael Sutherland, a tan and smooth Sinatra impersonator, can often be found at **La Scala Italian Bistro** in Dublin or **The Yard Club** in Hilliard suavely singing the Chairman of the Board's classics during his show, Sinatra and Friends. And if you find yourself there time and time again, you can hire Sutherland for your wedding or anniversary party. www.michaelsutherland.biz. **La Scala Italian Bistro, 4199 W. Dublin-Granville Rd., Dublin, 614-889-9431, www.lascalaitalianbistro.com or The Yard Club, 4065 Main St., Hilliard, 614-771-1400, www.yardclub.com.**

Get Cooking

For the price of a meal at a really good restaurant, get hands-on with your date with a cooking class at **Sur La Table** at Easton. Nearly any day of the week, you can learn to cook up Italian comfort foods or Parisian bistro food, among many other choices. Instructors include chefs from many of the area's best-known restaurants. *3990 Bond St. (at Easton), Columbus, 614-473-1211. www.surlatable.com.*

Skeeball for Sweeties

Maybe you grew up playing Pacman, or you just love to work out a little road rage on the driving machines. Either way there are a few locations around town where you can eat, drink and game the night away. On the west side, **Dave & Buster's** has all the interactive games you can think of in its "Million Dollar Midway," plus the classics such as billiards and Skeeball. You can also get a drink or a full meal in the restaurant, which is surprisingly good. *3665 Park Mill Run Dr., Hilliard, 614-771-1515, www.daveandbusters.com.*

On the east side, it's much the same at **GameWorks** at Easton, with more than 200 games and activities. The perk here may be the 18-and-older-only crowd after 10 p.m. and half price game play, cocktails and bar food on weekdays from 4-7 p.m. (attention cheap daters!). *165 Easton Town Center, Columbus, 614-428-7529, www.gameworks.com.*

For those who consider themselves a touch more upscale in the gaming arena, or just more in touch with sports, the **Buckeye Hall of Fame Café** not only features everything Ohio State from the Walk of Fame to the scarlet and gray décor, but it also provides plenty of gaming opportunities in the Arena Room, along with all of the food and drinks we've come to expect from these fun factories. *1421 Olentangy River Rd., Columbus, 614-291-2233, www.buckeyehalloffamecafe.com.*

Classically Romantic

Ah, a night at the **Ohio Theatre** listening to the classical music of Bach, Mozart or Beethoven beautifully played by the musicians of the **Columbus Symphony Orchestra**. For those unaccustomed to the Ohio Theatre, the sights in the historic downtown landmark alone are worth the price of admission. Add the sounds of the symphony and you have one delightful date. Beginning each September, the CSO kicks off a 47-week season, with packages of similarly themed concerts. During the summer, surround yourselves with the symphony during **Picnic with the Pops** on the lawn of Chemical Abstracts (off Olentangy River Rd. near OSU). Bring a blanket and sit on the lawn or purchase a four-seater table, which can be catered. You can wine, dine, listen to the symphony and even watch the stars. *39 E. State St., Columbus, 614-228-8600, www.columbussymphony.com, www.picnicwiththepops.com.*

A New Way to Cabaret!

For a boisterous and ballsy night out, check out the comic antics and rock-n-roll stylings of the **Shadowbox Cabaret**. Much like *Saturday Night Live*, skits at Shadowbox can sink or satisfy, but the house band, BillWho?, is always right on target with its energetic covers. For those not wanting to risk embarrassment, don't tell your server this is your first time at the 'Box. Virgins are singled out to the crowd! The cabaret features two-hour shows, with alcoholic beverages and appetizers available for order before the show or during intermission. *164 Easton Town Center, Columbus, 614-416-7625, www.shadowboxcabaret.com. Check Web site for show times.*

Celluloid Surprise

Want to really impress your date? Then rent a whole theater at the **Arena Grand** just for the two of you, complete with leather seats with center arms that lift up to create your own loveseat. For a few hundred dollars, depending on how long you rent the theater and any extras, you can rent the Screening Room and immerse yourself in anything from current releases to a DVD of your wedding to your favorite romantic flick (*Notorious* or *An Affair to Remember* anyone?). Have your meal or snacks catered from the theatre's bar and bistro. The staff will even arrange hotel accommodations for your special evening. *175 W. Nationwide Blvd., Columbus, 614-469-1074, www.arenagrand.com.*

Don't have the funds to rent a theater? There are still unique screening options in the city. **The Drexel** (all locations) and **Wexner Center** both offer limited-engagement viewings of alternative independent movies and documentaries you won't see coming soon to a Columbus megaplex. Film offerings might include a new print of *Metropolis* or a "mid-career retrospective" mini film festival for independent and mainstream directors such as Todd Haynes or Philip Kaufman. You might even catch a few premieres. Plus don't miss the Wexner's annual Ohio Short Film/Video Showcase every spring. *Drexel Theatres, see Web site, www.drexel.net, for a listing of the three locations; Wexner Center for the Arts, 1871 N. High St., Columbus, 614-292-3535, www.wexarts.org.*

ADVENTURE DATES

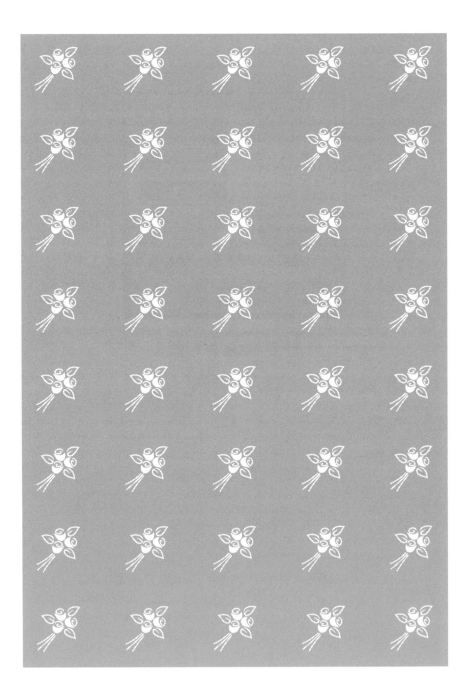

With its flat terrain and lack of ocean front property, Columbus isn't usually thought of as an adventure hot spot. What the city lacks in mountain climbing opportunities and surf adventures, however, it makes up for in other slightly less death-defying excitement.

From free sailboat rides to luxury hot air balloon tours, we've selected an assortment of activities to suit any adventurer's budget. Most activities can be done with little or no special equipment, or with gear that can be rented on site. Budgets and equipment needs are just a few things to consider before marrying romance and adventure. What may be a dangerous activity for some couples is just a fun sport for others. Laid back lovers may opt for a gentle moonlight horseback ride while high-action honeys may choose to get sporty and sweaty mountain biking through the woods. Whatever route you choose, spending time together doing something you both find challenging, exciting or new makes for a great date, even if it doesn't end with a romantic walk on the beach.

Special Tip: Make sure you and your date are compatible for an adventure date. It's not much fun to collect all the gear required to go on an adventure date only to have the other person whine about bug bites, sun burns or sweat. Before you go, make sure it's something you both want to do and consider how much time the date will take.

Bubbly Balloon Rides

Watch the earth seemingly fall away as you and your date ascend in a romantic hot-air balloon ride high above central Ohio. For daters with deep pockets, **Flying Colours Hot Air Balloons** offers Champagne Flights for couples. A call from the crew starts your morning and then it's off to watch them unpack and bring the balloon to life at one of the Delaware or Union County launch sites. Before departure, the crew offers a preflight briefing while you prep your camera for capturing some amazing views (or calm any proposal or pre-flight jitters). For about an hour, the two of you can sail in the ballooner's basket just above the treetops or thousands of feet into the air. As the balloon floats with the whim of the wind, a ground crew keeps in constant contact with the pilot. After touch down, the bubbly flows at a post-flight celebration where a traditional ballooner's toast is offered. The crew returns passengers to the launch site and suggests riders allow three to four hours for the entire experience. Launches are weather dependent and typically offered May through the end of September. *383 Breevort Rd., Columbus, 614-447-8684, www.flyingcoloursballoons.com.*

Sweetheart Spook

Couples have used scary movies as a way to snuggle close together since Lon Chaney's performance as the Phantom of the Opera in 1925. So imagine how close you and a date can get when you go on a Ghost Hunt at the **Ohio State Reformatory** in Mansfield. The multistory stone former prison (known more famously as the film site of *The Shawshank Redemption*) hosts Ghost Hunts various Friday and Saturday evenings from April through November. Hunters (age 21 and over only) enter the prison at 8 p.m. not to emerge until dawn—or sooner for those faint of heart. Each hunt includes a brief escorted tour. After that, you're on your own to wander the cell blocks, hoping to catch a glimpse of a former inmate who died in "The Hole" or record an eerie conversation coming from the warden's quarters between the boss and his wife. Stay together, because only a flashlight will light your way and the reformatory is known for its narrow passages, flights of stairs, and even a few holes in the floors. There is also a chill in the air inside the old structure (typically 10 degrees less than the outside temperature), but if a former inmate brushes past, you might feel more of an icy blast. Serious hunters are encouraged to bring thermometers to record unexpected temperature changes and compasses for documenting shifting magnetic fields. When you're ready for a jailbreak, the evening also includes a pizza and pop dinner. *100 Reformatory Rd., Mansfield, 419-522-2644, www.mrps.org.*

Hockey Dates and Figure Eights

Want to play a sport with your date, but don't want to commit to a league? Body checks and penalty boxes may not sound like the perfect combination for a *romantic* date, but for an icy *adventure* date, get physical during an adult pick-up game of ice hockey. The co-ed drop-in games at the Easton, Dublin, North and Dispatch Ice Haus **Chiller** locations are $12 per person, with a limit of 30 players. The matches, each lasting about two hours, are held at various times and require registration the day of the game. Afterward, massage away any bumps and bruises or, season permitting, take in a real NHL game with the **Columbus Blue Jackets**. Make sure you get caught on the roving CBJ "Kiss Cam." *Ice Haus, 200 W. Nationwide Blvd., Columbus, 614-246-3380, www.thechiller.com. (Check the Web site for a complete listing of dates and locations.)*

For those less inclined to combine sticks and skates, slow things down with an adults-only skate at the **Ohio State University Ice Rink**. Beginners can practice figure eights without the watchful eyes of young teens circling about doing their best Michelle Kwan performances. Public skating times vary by month, but an adult-only skate is usually held weekdays from 11:30 a.m.–12 p.m. and one Saturday evening per month at the recently renovated and modernized ice rink. Skate and locker rental is available for a modest fee. *390 Woody Hayes Dr., Columbus, 614-292-4154, ohiostatebuckeyes.collegesports.com/facilities/icerink.html.*

Moonlight Rides

Americans have a love affair with horses and even folks from a so-called "Cowtown" can appreciate the equine. With the full moon to light your way, saddle up one of the gentle steeds at **Stone Valley Ranch** for a nighttime ramble through the 400-plus acre ranch. The guided five-mile Moonlight Excursions are conducted the night of the full moon and two nights before and after, weather dependent. Experienced and novice riders alike can take in the moon-kissed views of creeksides, meadows, ridges and the hilltops the Hocking Hills region is so known for. Hold hands with your beloved as you admire the full moon in one of Ohio's most beautiful settings. After the one-hour ride, horsemen and women are treated to a bonfire, complete with snacks and hot dogs for roasting. *31606 Fairview Rd., Logan, 800-866-5196, www.hockinghillshorses.com.*

Getting Nautical

It's hard to imagine sailing in central Ohio, but out on the depths of Alum Creek Lake, couples can learn port from starboard with the **Alum Creek Sailing Association**. From May through October, the association offers six-week courses on Thursday nights and Sundays. Novice sailors receive about two and a half hours of instruction each week, which includes time aboard a 22- to 26-foot sailing boat and work in the classroom. If cruising the Alum Creek seas for weekly training is more of an enlistment than your relationship can handle, join the association Wednesday evenings during the sailing season, which runs April through October. Meet at the marina between 5:30–5:45 p.m. (that's 17:30–17:45 in captain's speak) where skippers will add "moveable weight," or human cargo, to keep their vessels from tipping in the wind. You can help the crew compete against some two dozen other sailing ships during the association's weekly race at the reservoir. Plan on racing for an hour to an hour and a half. Riders are accepted for free on a first come, first aboard basis. *ACSA Marina at Alum Creek State Park off Lewis Center Rd., Lewis Center, 614-844-6638, www.alumcreeksailing.com.*

Sunsets and S'mores

Nothing beats camping for rolling several adventures into one overnight bag. Close to Columbus, **Alum Creek State Park** is the campsite of choice. But there's more to camping than tent pitching and s'mores roasting here. Lovers can mountain bike on more than 14 miles of trails, swim, sled, snowmobile, ice fish, boat, hike or even take in the 38 miles of bridle trails. This 4,600-plus acre park features wooded and sunny campsites, as well as some overlooking the massive reservoir. Alum Creek also offers three fully equipped rent-an-RV units or five camper cabins. Of course the park has nearly 300 campsites for those used to roughing it. *3615 S. Old State Rd., Delaware, 740-548-4631, www.ohiodnr.com/parks/.*

Further from home, **Hocking Hills State Park** is for couples who love to hike, study nature and enjoy a relaxing time away from the big city. There are about 150 campsites here, but outdoor enthusiasts also have the option of renting one of 40 air-conditioned (or gas heated) cottages, complete with a fireplace, kitchen, bath and screened porch for relaxing. The park also offers three camper cabins. Hiking in the park or on nearby cave trails is the area's premier draw, but adventurers can also go rappelling or rock climbing in the Hocking State Forest. Be sure to bring some Jiffy Pop or the fixings for s'mores after a long day on the trails. Pets are also welcome at some sites. *19852 St. Rte. 664 S., Logan, 740-385-6842, www.ohiodnr.com/parks/. Ohio State Parks reservations can also be made by calling 1-866-OHIOPARK.*

Couples with Compasses

Getting lost can really spark the friction between couples. But instead of getting mad because your partner riding shotgun doesn't know how to read a map, brush up on your map and compass skills together with an orienteering adventure. During the spring and fall seasons the **Central Ohio Orienteers** set up courses around the area, such as **Alley Park** in Lancaster or **Camp Lazarus** in Delaware, for people who want to hike, compass, map and trek through woods and open areas in search of controls. The controls, centered on a feature to be found—

such as a large boulder—are placed in a particular order. Once orienteers find the control, they punch their control card (with that control's special punch) to show they've found the specified feature. Adventure courses range in length from a few kilometers with five or six controls to multi-kilometer adventures with a dozen or more special features to be found. *CentralOhioorienteers.org.*

If this doesn't seem like enough of an adventure, ramp it up with rogaining—and we don't mean hair treatments. Rogaining has been called extreme orienteering, with courses ranging in length from six, 12 or 24-hour events. Because rogaining is a scored sport instead of timed (participants get points for controls found) even novices can participate. Several rogaining events are held in the state, usually in southern Ohio locations such as **Zaleski State Park**, including upside down rogaines, which begin at sunset sending participants racing through the dark. *americanbushwhackingclub.org.*

A Bike Tour Built for Two

Biking is just the answer if you've spent too much time cuddling with your couch potato and want to see central Ohio. Westerville has an entire bikeway/leisure path loop system with various bikeways, while Dublin maintains more than 60 miles of bike paths, adding additional routes each year. *www.ci.westerville.oh.us/bikeways.asp or www.dublin.oh.us/quality/bikepath/.*

The Ohio Department of Natural Resources suggests the four following bicycle trails for viewing fall foliage, but hitting the trails is great whenever the weather allows. Perhaps the most popular bike zone in central Ohio is the **Olentangy Scioto River Bikeway**, which is 20 miles of scenic river views passing through everything from Berliner Park to the edge of downtown and Whetstone Park to Worthington Hills Park near the Delaware County line. Two trails in Licking County also top the ODNR's suggested list: the 14.3-mile **T.J. Evans Trail** between Johnstown and Newark and the 4.2-mile **Blackhand Trail** that runs through the Blackhand Gorge State Nature Preserve. Lovers wanting a slower cycle might enjoy the **Alum Creek State Park** 2-mile south multipurpose trail. *www.dnr.ohio.gov/fallcolor/bikes.htm.*

Don't confuse this Alum Creek trail with the Central Ohio Mountain Biking Organization's (COMBO) mountain bike trails, also at the Alum Creek State Park. Or for a really rugged ride, check out COMBO's looping trail at the **AEP ReCreation Lands** southeast of Zanesville. *www.joinomba.org/combo.*

Once you've felt the burn and want to turn your leisure time together into a competition, try one of Ohio's annual biking events such as the **Across Ohio Bicycle Adventure** (XOBA) that takes riders from border to border across Ohio on a different route each year, or the nation's largest bicycling touring weekend, **Tour of the Scioto River Valley** (TOSRV). *For a complete listing, see the Ohio Bicycle Events Calendar, www.ohiocycling.info/.*

Rowing on the River

Venetians inspire our romantic notions of relaxing water journeys with their glorious gondola rides through picturesque canals. Central Ohio doesn't have working canals anymore, or gondoliers. However, romance on the water is still alive and well. Each canoe season, roughly April through October, couples can paddle to the classics during one of the **Hocking Valley Canoe Livery's** Torch Light Tours. Tiki torches glow from the back of the canoes as couples paddle down the Hocking River while listening to classically trained opera singers or live blue-grass, country or traditional mountain music. At the end of the one to two-hour tour, couples can enjoy a bonfire and hot dog roast. For more natural lighting, partake of the livery's Moonlight Canoe rides, which also feature a variety of live entertainment. Afterward, sing around the campfire and enjoy marshmallows, a complementary glass of wine and general merriment under the stars. *31251 Chieftain Dr., Logan, 800-686-0386, www.hockinghillscanoeing.com/canoe.htm.*

The **Hocking Hills Canoe Livery at Rempel's Grove** also offers Moonlight Tours several times a year around the time of the full moon. The moonlight rides feature a bonfire and marshmallow roast afterward. Of course, canoeing in the daylight is also fun. Novices can take the five-mile Crockett's Trip or try the Lower Hocking Trip for more than 10 miles and 4–6 hours of adventure. Afterward, stop in to pet the goats and deer at the grove's free petting zoo or try some wonderful desserts at the Olde Dutch Restaurant right in front of the livery. *12789 St. Rte. 664 S., Logan, 800-634-6820, www.hockingriver.com.*

Xtreme Fun

Sometimes new and exciting love can make us feel like a teenager again. Maybe you've passed by your local skatepark and just thought how exciting it would be to go vert and get totally rad on a half pipe. Or maybe you've thought of what a long wait in the emergency room can feel like. Either way, recapture some of that liberating zeal that comes with being a kid again. Because skateparks are designed with youth in mind, we suggest sneaking in while the kiddies are at school. Start off in the beginner area at Dublin's **Coffman Skatepark**. The street style area is enclosed with three- to five-foot high banks and includes slider rails, steps and two-foot raised walls. There are also intermediate and advanced areas when your skills are ready. *Coffman Park Dr., south of Coffman Park Pavilion, Dublin, www.Dublin.oh.us/quality/skatepark.*

Reynoldsburg's **Kennedy Park** got top nods in one *Columbus Monthly* survey of local skateparks and Columbus' **Dodge Skateboard Park** is considered one of the oldest east of the Mississippi; it features a concrete basin. *7232 E. Main St., Reynoldsburg, 614-322-6806, www.ci.Reynoldsburg.oh.us/park_rec.html. 667 Sullivant Ave., 614-645-3388, www.columbusrecparks.com.* After riding the slider rails, regain some dignity with an in-line skate together like real adults.

Fun in the Bluff

Imagine the sun rising as you and your beloved watch the graceful movements of waterfowl, dipping their heads below the surface for a quick breakfast, while the two of you drink coffee snuggled in a viewing shelter. Or perhaps you would like to join the Columbus Audubon Society on a field trip for warbler watching at **Highbanks Metro Park**, a birdwalk through **Green Lawn Cemetery** or birding by canoe or

More Outdoor Pursuits

Whether you are interested in backpacking, rock climbing, caving, hiking, bicycling, canoeing, kayaking, rafting or winter activities, **Columbus Outdoor Pursuits** offers a wide selection of classes, trips and tours. The non-profit organization provides recreational and educational opportunities to youth and adult members. A wide variety of classes include river rescue, compass class, wilderness first aid, beginner's caving and rock climbing orientation. Members pay a nominal annual membership fee with member benefits including class priority and equipment rental options. **1525 Bethel Rd., Columbus, 614-442-7901, www.outdoor-pursuits.org/.**

kayak during the society's annual trek to **Twin Lakes Nature Preserve** in southern Delaware County. Whatever the field trip (they are conducted throughout the year), society members will be there to help you distinguish a duck from a goose. *P.O. Box 141350, Columbus, 740-549-0333, www.columbusaudubon.org.*

If you prefer birding as a couple's activity instead of a group outing, take some binoculars and a field guide to any one of the Metro Parks. **Pickerington Ponds** is known as the "bird watchers headquarters" with two observation areas, observation decks, a spotting scope and even a Watchable Wildlife designation. For maximum privacy try the **Wright Rd. Observation Area** where bird watchers can eye avian species from their cars. *7680 Wright Rd., Canal Winchester.* **Highbanks Metro Park** is another prime spot, with a viewing shelter off the wetland spur trail. In the winter, though, it's hard to beat bird watching from the comfort of the beautiful nature center. The collection of bird feeders, complete with microphones for indoor eavesdropping, creates a mecca for hungry birds. *9466 U.S. Rte. 23 N., Lewis Center, 614-508-8000, metroparks.net.*

PLACES
to STIMULATE
the MIND

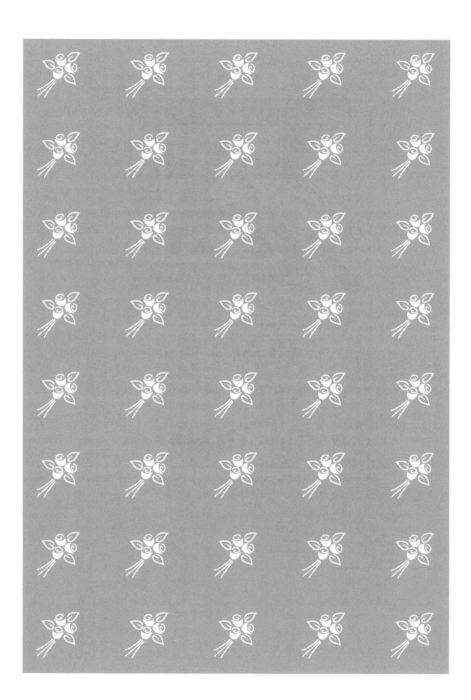

What's the sexiest part of any body? The mind! While someone's cute walk or sly smile may catch your eye, it's typically their mind that captures your heart. Like all parts of the body, the mind needs a good workout to stay in shape and workouts are always more fun with a partner. If you both like to learn new things, take a craft class at a local museum or listen to an artist's lecture at an arts center. The literary-minded might try an open mic poetry night or a summer literary picnic. Or maybe you would prefer a night of local theater or even listening to an architect elaborating on his designs and ideas. There are so many options out there to try and new things to learn, if you but put your mind to it! Your date might even find you a little sexier for it.

Literary Love

Columbus takes great pride in the fact that humorist and author James Thurber once lived and worked in our fair city. Walter Mitty fans and those who love Thurber's simply drawn cartoons can still tour **Thurber House**, the home that inspired Thurber's short story, "The Night the Ghost Got In." For a mind-stimulating date, though, we suggest signing up for one of the Evenings with Authors events or taking in a Summer Literary Picnic. The house hosts national award-winning authors and local talent during these popular evening events and picnics. Although you can purchase a reading-only ticket for the picnics, we suggest going all out and buying a catered dinner ticket as well. It's stimulating for mind and stomach alike. Check Web site for a list of upcoming author visits and don't forget to bring a book to be signed. Past authors have included such literary luminaries as Garrison Keillor, Doris Kearns Goodwin and John Updike, among others. *77 Jefferson Ave., Columbus, 614-464-1032, www.thurberhouse.org.*

Art Affair

You don't have to go to a bigger city to appreciate the masters of the art world. **The Columbus Museum of Art** specializes in late 19th- and early 20th-century American and European modern art, with an assortment of masterworks by famed artists such as Monet, O'Keefe, Renoir, Picasso and Matisse. While admission to the museum is free on Sundays, there's a reason to save your visit for a Thursday night. During Meet Me @ the Museum each Thursday beginning at 6 p.m., couples can enjoy the exhibitions while taking in the sounds of jazz frequently performed by members of the Jazz Arts Group. These events feature a cash bar, appetizers, tours and special activities surrounding the current exhibition—everything from a buddhist tea ceremony to correspond to the *Circle of Bliss: Buddhist Meditational Art* exhibit to a screening of the film *Can Can* by Jean Renoir (painter Auguste Renoir's son) for the recent *Renoir's Women* show. If you must go during the day, treat your date to lunch at the Palette Café and top it off with one of their delicious cookies. *480 E. Broad St., Columbus, 614-221-6801 or 614-221-4848 (24-hour information), www.columbusmuseum.org. Closed Mondays.*

The Poetry Pub

The scene around Ohio State's campus has undergone a major renovation recently with the Gateway Project, but there are a few standard sites that have withstood the test of time. Most notably among them is **Larry's** in the north campus area. Started in the early 1920s as the Lawrence Grill, Larry's has been in the Paoletti family ever since. More than just a campus bar, Larry's is a Bohemian poetry platform. Every Monday night from October through mid-May, the Poetry Forum at Larry's hosts featured poets, followed by an open mic for the brave of heart. *2040 N. High St., Columbus, 614-299-6010, www.larrysbar.com.*

A Modern Love Affair

The Wexner Center for the Arts is everything a big city contemporary arts center should be: thought-provoking, daring and cool. After an extensive three-year renovation, the Wexner Center reopened with a bang: a well-curated, highly erotic and modern art exhibit (*Part Object Part Sculpture*); a film tribute to deceased French filmmaker Louis Malle including an interview with Candice Bergen, his former wife; a free two-day arts symposium that brought in art critics from around the country; and a Wexner Center co-produced theater performance, *SUPER VISION*, which combined digital animation, computer music, video and live performance. This is the kind of place you could take your date to every week and never be bored between all the films, lectures, author readings, dance, theater and music performances. Plus, gallery admission is now free. *1871 N. High St.(on the OSU campus), Columbus, 614-292-3535, www.wexarts.org.*

Something to Talk About

If you find yourself downtown with your love on a Thursday at noon, stroll over to the **Columbus Recreation and Parks Cultural Arts Center** for one of their weekly **Conversations & Coffee** gatherings. For an hour you can listen to an artist discuss his or her style, artwork, inspirations, etc., while you enjoy complimentary coffee. Or, you can pack a lunch and make it a brown bag date. Discussion leaders range from architects to painters, from sculptors to mixed media artists and just about everyone else in between. Check out the center's Web site for a schedule of featured artists. *139 W. Main St., Columbus, 614-645-7047, www.culturalartscenteronline.org.*

If politics and social policy are more your bag, plan a lunchtime date for one of the **Columbus Metropolitan Club's** regular Wednesday forums. Past topics have included arts funding, urban sprawl and other community, state and national issues. Lunches are typically held at the Athletic Club of Columbus from noon to 1:15 p.m. Pre-registration is required. *136 E. Broad St., 614-464-3220, www.columbusmetroclub.org.*

Thinkers' Theatre

New York has Broadway, we have North Broadway Street in Clintonville. Never fear, though, Columbus does have its own professional resident theatre (in fact, it's the only one in Ohio)—CATCO. Each season the **Contemporary American Theatre Company** performs some half-dozen shows ranging from performance classics such as *Cat on a Hot Tin Roof* to premier presentations in the Vern Riffe Center downtown. For those who really want to probe the play and get personal with the actors, theatregoers can attend a Talk Back Sunday. For the visually impaired, CATCO offers audio descriptions, with free headsets, the fourth Sunday of a performance run. When CATCO is off for the summer season, you can still catch some thinking-person's theatre with free **Shakespeare in the Park** performances by **Actors' Theatre** at Schiller Park in German Village. *CATCO, 77 S. High St., Columbus, 614-469-0939 (Box Office), www.catco.org; Actors' Theatre, 1000 City Park Ave., Columbus, 614-444-6888, www.theactorstheatre.org.*

Handmade from the Heart

Ladies love jewelry. Imagine how fun it would be to receive (or give) homemade jewelry crafted from the heart, or even a knitted scarf. During the **Ohio Craft Museum's** Craft View Nights, participants can learn a new skill at these after-work art parties that include meeting an artist, viewing the exhibits, snacks, and, of course, crafty time! Workshops run the gamut of Martha maneuvers from beading to jewelry to just about anything you could want to make and take. For more dedicated participants, the museum offers all-day workshops as well. Check Web site for class listings. *1665 W. Fifth Ave., Columbus, 614-486-4402, www.ohiocraft.org/museum.html. Closed Saturdays.*

ROMANTIC
GETAWAYS

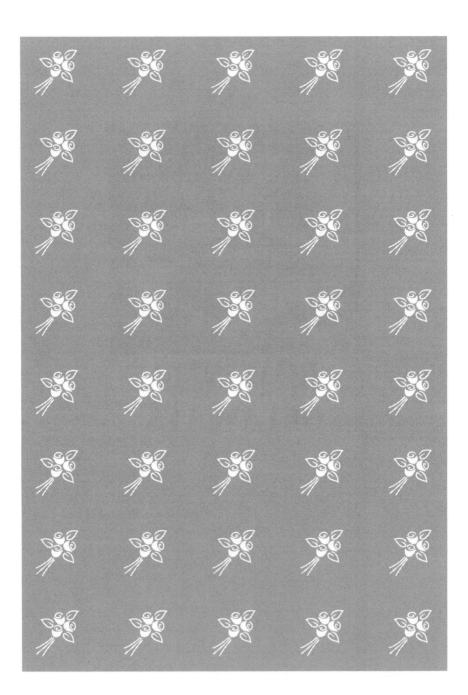

If you're finding it difficult to remember what your true love looks like, let alone feel inspired, you may need more than a night on the town to reconnect. Busy schedules and life's general harriedness can often get in the way of the best of romantic intentions. An in-town or weekend getaway can be just the thing for reviving the romance in your life. And the Columbus area has plenty of great places to do just that. Options include secluded, wooded retreats; full-service, four-star hotels; luxury country estates; and intimate, small town inns. Feeling a little daunted? Enlist the aid of the lodging's owners and staff. They are more than willing to help set the mood and bring a little moonlight back into your life.

Special Tip: Be sure to ask about packages geared for romance. For spur-of-the-moment getaways, sign up to be on the lodging's e-mail list. You'll find out about specials few know about, plus it makes it a lot easier to be spontaneous.

Best Reason for Sleeping In

Sometimes there's nothing better than sleeping in someone else's bed, particularly when the bed is clothed in 300-count thread Egyptian sheets and a warm but light-as-air duvet, as the beds are at the **Westin Great Southern Hotel**. The "Heavenly beds" at this restored Starwood property are arguably the best in the city and make for a great excuse to loll around with your lover. Sign up for Starwood's preferred guest program and, as available, you can get a 4 p.m. check-out. The addition of the on-site Marengo Institute spa ups the heavenly factor several notches. Couples can indulge in simultaneous pampering packages, which can include full body or hot stone massages, aromatherapy treatments, facials, manicures and pedicures, among many other deliciously decadent treatments. *614-224-6640, www.marengoinstitute.com.*

The Westin's prime downtown location between German Village, the Brewery District and Columbus' restored theaters makes it a great choice for a night of wining, dining and theater-going. Don't feel like wandering out? The attached **Southern Theatre** hosts some of the more interesting concerts in town. Everyone from violin virtuosos to folk singers have performed here. *www.capa.com/ohio.* Before retiring, have a nightcap in the newly redone, all warm wood Thurber's Bar, a nod to James Thurber, Columbus' patron saint of literary humor. *310 S. High St., Columbus, 614-228-3800, www.westin.com/columbus. Rates from $129.*

Highly Entertaining

The brick and Georgian facade of the **Hilton Easton** is reminiscent of a college campus, but it's a good bet that few college campuses have valets dressed in black to park your car upon arrival. Inside, this 300-room, four-star hotel exudes elegance with lots of marble, warm wood, original artwork adorning the walls and a lobby lounge complete with piano. Rooms on the upgraded club level floors include bathrobes, Italian marble bathrooms and access to the library-like concierge lounge, where each morning a Continental breakfast is served and each evening offers a cocktail hour. Order room service from the Dining

Room restaurant and your tray will arrive with a small vase of fresh flowers. Monday and Wednesday afternoons, you can partake in the Hilton's High Tea in the English tradition, with scones and cream, tea sandwiches and, of course, tea (reservations necessary).

Couples' massages can be arranged for the fitness center or your room. A concierge is readily available to help with any other requests, from dinner reservations to spa appointments at one of Easton's day spas to rose petals on the bed. Ask about special romance and shopping packages, which can include champagne and discounts to Easton stores. Plus packages can always be customized. "If we don't have it, we can make it up," says the concierge. *3900 Chagrin Dr., Columbus (across from Easton Town Center), 614-414-5000, www.hiltoncolumbus.com. Rates from $179.*

Perhaps the best reason to stay at the Hilton Easton are all the great date ideas, just steps from the hotel's doors. You can play video games at **GameWorks**, catch a flick or dine at any number of great restaurants. For outstanding ambiance try **Café Istanbul**, resembling a sultan's palace, or **Brio** for high Roman romance. During the holiday season you can take a romantic carriage ride for two and snuggle under the blanket together. In summer, listen to jazz concerts in the courtyard. Before you return to your hotel room, you might want to make a stop at the **Victoria's Secret** across from Smith and Wollensky. This VS store is one of the test stores for the nation, so you're likely to find lacy and racy things here that may not show up elsewhere. *www.eastontowncenter.com.*

A Modern Proposition

Perhaps the most modern and hip option for couples is the **Lofts Hotel**, a 44-room boutique hotel restored to resemble a loft in New York's SoHo. The contemporary, sleek rooms are outfitted with floor-to-ceiling windows, exposed brick walls, Italian sheets and Aveda bath products. The bathrooms build on the big-city theme with New York City subway tiles. This sophisticated hotel makes a great choice for wining and dining in the nearby **Arena District** or **Short North** arts district, just a few blocks away.

Romance packages here are particularly good. They can include rose-petal turn-down service, a Godiva chocolate nightcap, champagne, massages and breakfast in bed. A recent chocolate lovers package even added a souvenir copy of the mouth-watering DVD *Chocolat. 55 E. Nationwide Blvd., Columbus, 614-461-2663, www.55lofts.com. Rates from $169.*

Sexy Soaks

Several central Ohio lodging facilities offer rooms with whirlpools, Jacuzzis or hot tubs to sooth your muscles and set the mood for romance.

- **Homewood Suites at the Airport**, suites with fireplace and whirlpool. **2880 Airport Drive, Columbus, OH 43219, 614-428-8800, www.homewoodsuites.com.**
- **Glenlaurel**, private outdoor hot tubs complete with speakers built into the deck to listen to your favorite "In the mood" music. (See entry on page 84).
- **Cherry Valley Lodge**, 16 jacuzzi suites. (See entry on page 83).
- Plus for many of the cabins in Hocking Hills, hot tubs or whirlpools are de rigeur. For more ideas, go to **www.1800hocking.com.**
- **AmeriHost Inn & Suites Columbus at Rickenbacker, 2323 Port Rd., Columbus,** and **AmeriHost Inn & Suites Columbus Southeast, 6323 Prentiss School Rd., Canal Winchester, 800-434-5800, www.amerihostinns.com.** Large freestanding whirlpool suites with oversize towels and robes.

The Seeds of Love

There are many things to like about Newark's **Cherry Valley Lodge**—the attentive staff, the gazebo and duck pond filled courtyard, the roaring fireplace in the lobby, the stand-out restaurant—but our favorite just may be the bathtubs built for two, available in the inn's 200 typical rooms. Upgrade to one of 16 suites, and the tubs become jacuzzis.

The lodge's thoughtful extra touches include fluffy robes; bikes to take on the rails-to-trails path out the inn's back door; duck food for feeding the ducks; and benches placed discreetly all over the flower-filled grounds, allowing for plenty of hand-holding opportunities.

The lodge does several event weekends throughout the year, from mystery weekends to gourmet cooking classes, to wine tastings, a costume Halloween Ball and ballroom dancing weekends. For all-out romance try the romance package, which includes a stay in a luxury suite filled with a dozen candles, a rose petal path, champagne, chocolate covered strawberries and a couple's massage in your room or in the on-site spa. The lodge may even send you away with a pack of free black-eyed Susan seeds to keep you in the bloom of love, long after you've returned home. *2299 Cherry Valley Rd., Newark, 740-788-1200, 800-788-8008, www.cherryvalleylodge.com. Rates from $149.*

Hearts and Horses

Those in search of a relaxing, rural, romantic getaway, head for **Heartland Country Resort**, a luxury bed and breakfast favored by Mt. Vernon native and actor Paul Newman. The inn is located about an hour north of Columbus on 100-plus acres of rolling farmland, woods and meadows. Owner Dorene Henschen, a local elementary school teacher, wanted to give guests the same kind of country experiences she grew up with on her family farm in northwest Ohio. She's done just that with her inn. Guests can wander the woods and meadows, help with the daily farm chores or get a whole new perspective on the world by riding one of the inn's dozen-plus horses. The inn can create custom experiences for couples…candlelight dinners, private massages in your room, picnic lunches for a romp through the meadows.

For privacy, select one of the inn's suites in the secluded log cabin near the woods. They include cathedral ceilings, two-person jacuzzis, kitchenettes and private porches with swings. Particularly nice is the Woodland Suite, a warm, spacious suite decorated in lodge fashion with log walls and a corner hearth stove. A full breakfast is available in the inn's dining room or can be delivered to your room. If you're lucky, you'll get a chance to taste the specialty of the house: a creamy, cinnamon-flavored sour cream coffee cake. Horseback riding costs $25 per person for the first hour, $11 per person per half-hour after that. Novice riders can choose private lessons for an additional cost. *3020 Twp. Rd 190, Fredericktown, www.heartlandcountryresort.com, 800-230-7030 or 419-768-9300. Rates from $100.*

Great side trip idea: **Richland Carrousel Park** in Mansfield, an indoor carousel with intricately carved giraffes, horses, ostriches, a lion and more. Open 7 days, 11 a.m.–5 p.m. Take I-71 N. to U.S. Rte 30 W. to St. Rte. 13 S. (Main St.) *Downtown Mansfield at the corner of Fourth and Main sts., 419-522-4223, www.richlandcarrousel.com.*

A Poetic Interlude

Leave it to a poet to create a romantic world full of secret gardens, secret passageways and cottages and crofts on 140 acres full of waterfalls and woods. From the minute you enter the Scottish country inn **Glenlaurel** founded by poet Michael Daniels, you are lulled into a different world. Celtic music wafts through the rooms, and the fireplace in the main house glows. Forget about cell phone reception, *USA Today* or television. Everything in the crofts or cottages (all named after Scottish clans) is designed for comfort and conversation. Rooms come with elegant fluffy robes, hot tubs and built-in speakers on the deck and a fireplace, which in some rooms, is viewable from both the living room and the bedroom.

Inn dinners are an event in their own right. The typical five- to seven-course meals start with the Scottish tradition of the sound of pipes, followed by a reading of a piece by Scottish poet Robert Burns (famous for the line "O my luve's like a red, red rose..."). During the day, the staff at Glenlaurel can pack a picnic for two for your walk through the woods, fields or one of the nearby Hocking Hills parks. Or if you feel like cocooning, you can order romantic dinners delivered to your room.

Glenlaurel is one of the more interesting places to spend New Year's Eve. The inn's traditional Scottish New Year's known as Hogmanay, includes a gourmet dinner, during which each guest is asked to read a bit of their own poetry or the poetic fashionings of a favorite bard. Guests then proceed outside for a blazing bonfire, and enter back inside only after the "first-footer" spreads salt and coal on the entrance way for seasoning and warmth.

Photo courtesy Glenlaurel

Dining at Glenlaurel.

Stay at Glenlaurel during your anniversary, and you'll go home with a souvenir plate, specially designed for Glenlaurel each year by **Bluebird Pottery**, a potter based in the nearby artists' enclave of Amesville. The inn has won over so many guests, many of the regulars return for the holiday open house (typically one of the first weekends after Thanksgiving) to give tours of the cottages and crofts and even hand out their own treats. *14940 Mount Olive Rd., Rockbridge, 800-809-REST, www.glenlaurel.com. Rates from $119 in main house, and from $219 for crofts and cottages.*

Medieval Mystery

Two area inns are perfect for those who've dreamed of playing lord and lady of the manor. On the edge of Hocking Hills, high on a hill and up a steep and windy drive sits **Ravenwood Castle**, a bed and breakfast built to resemble a medieval village. While the castle was being built in the early 1990s, owner Sue Maxwell and her husband took a trip to England to look at doors, floors and other architectural details, and wound up modeling the wooden floor in the Great Hall after a copy of the floor pattern of the queen's bedroom at Greenwich Palace.

To enter the castle, you must cross over a wood drawbridge and then ring a bell and wait to be received. Lodging choices include fairy tale cottages, the castle's main rooms (with names such as King Arthur's Suite or the Henry VIII room) and unique gypsy wagons, available in the summer and featured as one of Rand McNally's seven most unique places to sleep in the U.S. All rooms have fireplaces and dramatic, handmade four-poster beds (made by a local pastor).

The first two weeks every February the B&B offers a "Sweetheart Serenade" package, which includes a dinner of aphrodisiac foods and serenading musicians. Throughout the year, you can catch one of the inn's mystery weekends, a whodunit costumed affair that will leave you feeling oh so Agatha Christie. *65666 Bethel Rd. (Off St. Rte. 93 and Bethel Rd. in Hocking Hills), 800-477-1541, 740-596-2606, www.ravenwoodcastle.com. Rates from $45 (gypsy wagons) or from $115 for rooms.*

You can also get away with your prince or princess to **Landoll's Mohican Castle,** a luxury inn located about an hour-plus north of Columbus in Mohican Country on 1,100 wooded acres. The castle suites and cottages have heated Italian tile floors, wall tapestries, overstuffed chairs and big beds. Amenities include a sauna, a game room and an indoor pool with a waterfall and small cave. Romantic extras include massages, picnic lunches, and depending on the season, cozy horse-drawn carriage or sleigh rides. *561 Twp. Rd. 3352, Loudonville, 800-291-5001, 419-994-3427, www.landollsmohicancastle.com. Rates from $190.*

What a Little Moonlight Can Do

Nature is the star of the show at the **Inn at Cedar Falls**, another romantic getaway in Hocking Hills. It's a great choice for couples looking to strip away the static of every day life. Lodging choices include rooms in the "barn" main lodge or restored 1840s log cabins in the woods or cottages. Rooms are decorated in a spare but welcoming style, with antiques and writing desks or tables for conversation and coffee. Most cottages and cabins come with whirlpool tubs, gas log stoves and decks for stargazing. As you walk around the woods and meadows, don't be surprised if Monday the cat follows you to your room.

The inn offers a variety of event weekends from nature photography workshops to wine tastings to couple's cooking classes with the head chef for the inn's on-site gourmet restaurant. Plan on having at least one meal in the restaurant (extra, but worth it). In winter, sit in the cozy indoor cabin, or during warmer months, enjoy a meal al fresco on the patio. *21190 St. Rte. 374, Logan, (From Columbus, take U.S. Rte 33 S. to St. Rte. 664 E. to St. Rte. 374), 800-65-FALLS, www.innatcedarfalls.com. Rates from $89.*

Grand in Granville

Two inns are worth a getaway to Granville, a nearby village that feels like a New England college town with its tree-lined streets, the requisite tall church steeple and main street shops complete with old-fashioned ice cream parlor, and of course, a college—Denison University. The Tudor-style **Granville Inn** is popular with politicians, including Indiana Senator Richard Lugar, a Denison alum, who often stays in one of the rooms in the old girl's school Seminary wing. All rooms are different, but most have queen or king-size beds and pull-out sofas. Couples who emerge for dinner should reserve a table by the fireplace in the restaurant. *314 E. Broadway, Granville 740-587-3333, 888-472-6855, www.granvilleinn.com. Rates from $99.*

Across the street from the Granville Inn sits the **Buxton Inn**, a pink painted historic inn known for its on-site restaurant, two-story porches and formal gardens. Rooms at the old tavern-like Buxton range from intimate to gold and grand. If you feel a little chill during your stay it just may be one of the inn's resident ghosts who reportedly haunt the historic inn. All the more reason for cuddling close together. *313 E. Broadway, Granville, 740-587-0001, www.buxtoninn.com. Rates from $80.*

A Lover's Packing List

Besides the wow 'em unmentionables, here are a few more ideas to stow in your overnight bag and set the mood.

- bubble bath for a relaxing soak
- massage oil
- books of poetry (Billy Collins, Yeats and Theodore Roethke are good choices) or humorous books to read to each other and get the endorphins going (anything by Garrison Keillor, Bill Bryson or Steve Martin should do the trick).
- music: try the soundtrack from *Big Night* (a collection of songs by classic Italian crooners from the '50s and '60s), or Madeleine Peyroux, a modern jazz singer whose smoky voice sounds amazingly similar to Billie Holiday (also a good classic choice).
- a sketchbook, charcoal and drawing pencils for capturing each other in time. The nonartistically inclined can still have a good time with this, making it a "what's that?" Pictionary guessing game. Or see what fun you can have with a digital camera.

CHEAP
(& Romantic)
DATES

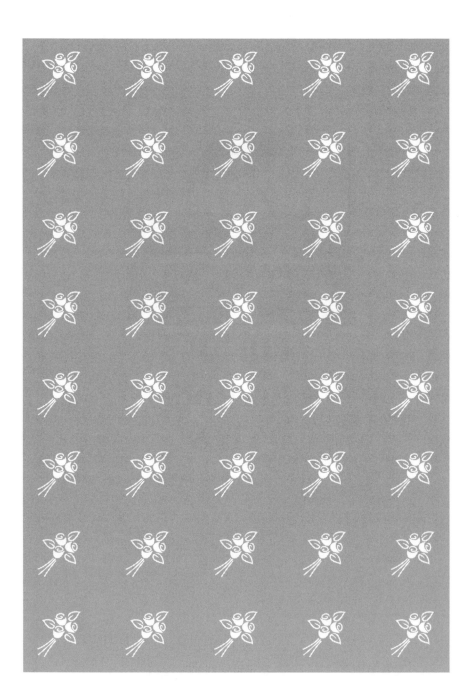

A lot of dating takes place in our young adult lives when our eyes are typically bigger than our budgets. We admit to our fair share of student-discount movie tickets and homemade dinners in front of an apartment TV set. But just because the budget is feeling a little strained, it doesn't mean you have to stay in for fun or be "cheap." We prefer to think of "cheap" dates as inexpensive outings that don't break the bank, not afterthought outings because you're still searching the couch for change. After all, there's nothing romantic about debt.

Fortunately, there are lots of ways to enjoy time with your date in Columbus for less than the price of cinema admission. Whether you want to enjoy a moonlit walk or a picnic in the park, the options are as bountiful as your imagination. For those in a creative rut, though, we've highlighted some of our favorite cheap dates.

Tropical Columbus

Have you promised your date the world when your wallet is as flat as a map? Tour the Earth's biomes at the **Franklin Park Conservatory** instead. Located off Broad Street just east of downtown, the conservatory is a plant oasis near the heart of the concrete jungle. Outside the conservatory, five acres of gardens welcome visitors, but the main attraction is inside the building. Begin your journey in the Himalayan Mountains room, following the paved path until you reach the Rain Forest. Inside the forest's lush environs an assortment of plants and a few creatures reside, such as a colony of leaf-cutter ants and a pair of tropical birds. Next door, cacti grow in the desert room, while iguanas lounge on branches in their adobe home. Perhaps the most popular area, the Pacific Islands room is an indoor fantasyland of flowing water, glorious plants and, for several months each year, a beautiful collection of free-flying butterflies. If you prefer larger flying spectacles, feed the colorful lories in their home next door to the islands. Other must-see areas of the conservatory include the succulent patio, bonsai courtyard, and palm room. The Conservatory has also taken to featuring art among the atmospheres, acquiring several Dale Chihuly glass pieces in its permanent collection. When special displays such as these are on view, this is like two dates in one! *1777 E. Broad St., Columbus, 614-645-TREE, www.fpconservatory.org.*

Sweets with your Sweet

After fixing your loved one a spectacular at-home meal—or a somewhat unforgettable supper—head to **Mozart's Bakery and Piano Café** for the meal's grand finale. While a slice of after-dinner heaven at any one of Columbus' popular restaurants will set diners back around five dollars just for the dessert, Mozart's offers a delectable assortment of European and American desserts that typically cost less than three dollars, with some just under a buck. Whether you crave a cannoli, fruit flan, petit fours, torte or even the beautiful Austrian peach (as pretty as it is palatable), there is sure to be something to love. We prefer the light and fluffy cheesecake with fresh fruit topping, but will gladly lick the plate of any offering. For an added touch of romance, classical musi-cians play the baby grand piano Friday and Saturday nights in the café's subdued setting. You'll feel like you've blown the budget all for $10 or so if you throw in some drinks. Or make your own coffee and surprise your sweet with a take-out selection of desserts to be enjoyed at home in front of the fireplace. *2885 N. High St., Columbus, 614-268-3687, mozartscafe.com. Check Web site for additional area locations.*

A French Picnic

Just beyond Columbus' main library, people lounge along the banks of the **Topiary Garden's** pond, enjoying its eight boats and accompanying dogs, cat and monkey during beautiful afternoons. Actually, they are topiary people, as are the other features—except for the pond, which is real—portraying Georges Seurat's Impressionist painting *A Sunday Afternoon on the Island of La Grand Jatte.* Begin your date at the park's southeast corner, near the gatehouse, to view the living "painting" as Seurat would have seen it. Imagine the pond as the River Seine while watching the sweet autumn clematis flutter gently in the breeze. For those unfamiliar with Seurat's original work, a reproduction is available for visual comparison.

Such a spectacular, and free, setting from sunrise to sunset is only enhanced by a prepared picnic to be enjoyed among the landscape or on one of the park's picnic tables or benches. Celebrate the French artist's life (and the view of France's northern river) with a loaf of crusty French bread and an assortment of French cheeses and chocolate. Or for the more budget conscious, try some homemade French toast or crepes for a morning treat. For discreet picnickers, a quick French kiss might also be in order. While picnicking, search for the cat hidden among the topiaries, which is not part of the original painting. From April through December, park visitors can also enjoy **Yewtopia on Town**, the park's chateau-style museum shop and visitor's center. Browsing is always free, and it gives you an excuse to linger. *Corner of E. Town St. and Washington Ave., Columbus, 614-645-0197, www.topiarygarden.org.*

BYOB Painting Party

Demi Moore and Patrick Swayze made crafting clay sexy in *Ghost*. You won't get your hands wet on the potter's wheel, but you can splash some paint on pre-made items during **Art & Clay on Main's** Friday night date nights in Lancaster. Each Friday night from 6–10 p.m. two adults can paint for the studio time of one in this trendy downtown studio with an urban revival flare. Artists can choose options from traditional plate and cup pieces to light switch covers and holiday figurines. The helpful staff can show you how to work with the sponges and color selections, as well as any special stencils or other embellishments. If you can't determine the look of your piece, cozy up on one of the couches and leaf through the studio's assortment of art books. Did we mention that dates can bring their own beverages to date night? *150 W. Main St., Lancaster, 740-653-1755, www.artclayonmain.com.*

Love Between the Covers (Of books, that is!)

If your idea of a good date is some mental stimulation at a low price, then you're in luck because Columbus has a variety of good discount bookstores from **Karen Wickliff Books** on High Street to **The Library Store** at the main Columbus Public Library. While **Half Price Books** is a chain store, and we generally like to eschew the pedestrian on a unique low-cost date, you can't argue with the three local stores' prices—half off used paperbacks and discounts on used and overstocked books, magazines, music and movies. For this chain's best local selection, check out the Upper Arlington store, which is the most spacious and well stocked. *1375 W. Lane Ave., Upper Arlington, 614-486-8765, www.halfpricebooks.com.*

When it comes to huge, deeply discounted inventories, the largest is the **Village Bookshop** near Linworth in northwest Columbus. Housed in the former Linworth United Methodist Church, low-cost book seekers praise the shop's large assortment of overstocked, new, used and out-of-print books. From Civil War books and memorabilia to cooking, science fiction, archaeology and the arts, this is the place to come and browse a while, preferably while snuggled next to your date in one of the store's lounge areas. *2424 W. Dublin-Granville Rd., Columbus, 614-889-2674.*

Picnics: The Versatile Low Cost Date

Picnics are a great low-cost date because you can set your own budget and handpick the atmosphere you want. Columbus offers a variety of great picnic spots, from the **Topiary Garden** (see French Picnic entry, pg. 93) downtown to **Highbanks Metro Park** north of I-270. For a people-watching picnic, dine along the banks of **Ohio State University's Mirror Lake**, among the roses at the **Park of Roses**, or under the grand trees at **Goodale Park** in Victorian Village. Whatever the location, remember to take along a blanket for reposing and plenty of foods that look fancy but are easy to make, such as chocolate-dipped strawberries and finger sandwiches.

If being close to your loved one while book shopping is what you seek, try German Village's **The Book Loft** packed with 32 rooms of new, discounted books. This is not a used bookstore, but some of the discounts will make you think otherwise. With its labyrinth of rooms, the store that stretches across a city block is best navigated with the help of one of the Loft's maps and its frequently consulted directional signs. Each room plays its own mood music and somewhere among the stacks, the Loft's cat is just waiting to be scratched. *631 S. Third St., Columbus, 614-464-1774, www.bookloft.com/indexn.htm.*

Chocolate Fantasy

Because chocolates are so significantly entwined with dating, especially on Valentine's and Sweetest Days, why not take a free tour of the **Anthony-Thomas Candy** factory? On Tuesdays and Thursdays from 9:30 a.m. to 2:30 p.m. one-hour guided tours take guests from candy making to final packing. Visitors are guided along glass-enclosed catwalks to take in the factory's sights and smells. The tour ends, quite naturally, in the confectionary shop, where you can purchase such temptations as chocolate-covered cherries. *1777 Arlingate Lane, Columbus, 614-272-9221 or 877-226-3921, www.anthony-thomas.com.*

High Brow Art on a Low Brow Budget

There's something sexy about art appreciation with the one you love. Maybe it's the good lighting, quiet atmosphere, and works to appreciate, but Columbus' art scene is alive and, for the most part, free. Just off the No. 2 bus line (in case transportation is also a budget issue) is the **Ohio Arts Council's Riffe Gallery**, a showcase of Ohio and international artistic talents. From paintings and photography to jewelry and metal work, the Riffe runs the gamut of exhibits, all for free. *77 S. High St., Columbus, 614-644-9624, www.oac.state.oh.us/riffe.*

Close to downtown, **The King Arts Complex** provides art exhibitions in the **Elijah Pierce Gallery**, emphasizing works by African-American artists. The art exhibitions are virtually free— $2 donation per adult—and the complex also offers a variety of dance performances, jazz concerts, musicals, poetry readings and other artistic offerings, all at affordable prices. *867 Mt. Vernon Ave., Columbus, 614-645-KING, www.kingartscomplex.com. Closed Sundays and Mondays.*

After a downtown tour, catch the No. 2 back up High Street to the **Wexner Center for the Arts** on the Ohio State University campus. It's a multidisciplinary arts center with a modern edge, also with free exhibitions. On certain days, guided walk-in tours of the exhibits are also offered for free. *1871 N. High St., Columbus, 614-292-3535, www.wexarts.org.*

For fine crafts, the **Ohio Craft Museum** offers five major exhibits annually, all at no cost. Past exhibits have showcased contemporary American rugs, pottery, weaving and garden art. *1665 W. Fifth Ave., Columbus, 614-486-4402, www.ohiocraft.org.*

People Watching & Gallery Hopping

For more than 20 years, people have gathered the first Saturday of each month for the **Short North Arts District's Gallery Hop**. The Hop, which stretches along High Street from Poplar Street to Fifth Avenue, is a shopping, dining, people watching, art admiring affair. Particularly in the summer, when the events are also known as Hot Hops, the crowds come out en masse to take in everything from vintage clothing shops and leather fetish stores to upper-crust art sculptures and high-end antiques. The Hops usually feature exhibit openings, artist receptions and lots of quirky people and places. And, of course, it's all free. While there are several fine dining options along the route, such as **Martini** and **L'Antibes**, there are also eateries for those with a budget on a diet, such as **The Coffee Table** or **Phillips and Son Coney Island**. *N. High St., Columbus, 614-228-0850, www.shortnorth.org.*

Share the Love

Exploring your interests and finding out about each other is one of the joys of dating. And volunteering together is one way to share your skills and find out what the two of you are really passionate about, besides each other. From giving assistance at an American Red Cross blood drive to walking dogs for the Humane Society, **FIRSTLINK** can connect you with some 800 non-profit organizations that suit your talents and interests. Of course volunteer work isn't just for special-cause organizations. The arts need free help too. CATCO, CAPA, The King Arts Complex, and Wexner Center for the Arts all accept volunteers for their usher corps, and you'll probably get to take in a free show on the job—not a bad perk if you don't mind standing through the program. FIRSTLINK lists cultural arts volunteer needs in organizations from Actors' Theatre to Zivili, and also special events volunteer gigs such as workers for First

Night Columbus. So whether you want to enjoy a festival for free or volunteer in an office on an ongoing basis, these are the people to call. *195 N. Grant Ave., Columbus, 614-221-6766, www.firstlink.org.*

German Village: Old World Columbus

We'd all love to have enough money to fly to Europe on a whim, just to enjoy a romantic evening along the cobbled streetscape of a quaint town. For many of us that dream is a bit out of touch with our wallets, but Columbus does provide an alternative: **German Village**. Founded in the early 19th century by local brick masons, brewery workers and carpenters, the village is an homage to the European home these German immigrants left behind. Strolling along the brick-lined sidewalks while admiring the beautifully renovated cottages tucked side by side is a nice date in itself, but the area also offers other low-cost attractions, such as free Shakespeare in the Park on summer evenings at **Schiller Park** and an eclectic mix of shops for browsing. For bargain hunters, each year the area hosts Columbus' largest yard sale, **Village Valuables**. It's almost as well known as the annual **Oktoberfest** held every fall, which is a celebration of music, food and beer. **German Village Society, 588 S. Third St., Columbus, 614-221-8888, www.germanvillage.org**.

Bowling Balls & Slyder Squares

Sometimes you just have to admit that the budget doesn't allow for expensive evenings out. So embrace your cheap side for an evening of fun at the bowling alley. Whether you enjoy bowling early on a Sunday morning or during the wee hours of Wednesday night, **Columbus Square Bowling Palace**, stationed on the back side of a strip mall off St. Rte. 161, is open 24 hours a day, seven days a week. While bowling during peak hours will set you back less than five bucks per person per game—which is pretty low cost—the Palace offers even better rates during off times, such as week-night three-hour blocks from midnight to 3 a.m. for $10.50 per person or Sunday morning blocks from 9 a.m. to noon for $9.50 per person. *5707 Forest Hills Blvd., Columbus, 614-895-1122, www.palacelanes.com.*

And whatever time you finish bowling, there are sure to be more than a dozen local **White Castle** restaurants open and serving coffee, burgers or even onion rings. The chain, based in Columbus, is best known for its 2$1/2$-inch square burgers known as Slyders is always popular with the after-bar crowd, but that doesn't mean you can't go after bowling, too. *www.whitecastle.com.*

If burgers doused in onions don't sound appealing at 7 a.m., go to another off-hours favorite: **Tee Jaye's Country Place** restaurants. The food at the eight local eateries is down-home cooking, with generous helpings of gravy. There's even a location near the Bowling Palace. *1264 E. Dublin-Granville Rd., Columbus, 614-885-7537.*

Stargazer's Delight

With the constant glare of city lights it's hard to see the big sky above us. If you're lucky enough to live where the nighttime sky still comes to visit, then plan a date out in the elements and see who can wish on the first falling star. Impress your date with vast amounts of planetary knowledge by borrowing a constellation book from the library. Or, for less than $10 per person, you can let the experts tell you what is out there. Nearly every Friday and Saturday night people gather at the **Perkins Observatory** in Delaware County—Ohio's only observatory offering hundreds of public programs annually—for astronomy talks, a planetarium show and, of course, gazing through the telescopes. The Observatory recommends purchasing reserve tickets in advance or calling one to two hours before the program starts the day you plan to visit for ticket availability. *U.S. Rte. 23, Delaware, 1/4 mile south of St. Rte. 315, 740-363-1257, www.perkins-observatory.org.*

Somewhere in the **Metro Parks** system, when the moon is full, there is almost certain to be a full-moon hike. Whether you want to shuffle through the snow on a brisk walk or listen to the sounds of the nightlife during a summer hike, there are a variety of full-moon walks to choose from. And like almost all Metro Parks offerings, the walks are free. *Main office, 1069 W. Main St., Westerville, 614-508-8000 (24-hour information) or 614-891-0700 (main office), www.metroparks.net.*

Bogey and Bacall on a Budget

Humphrey Bogart, Lauren Bacall, Spencer Tracy and Grace Kelly—their very images just ooze Hollywood glamour and romance. Sure, you can pick up a classic movie on DVD at any local library, but to really appreciate love on the silver screen in an equally timeless setting, try the **CAPA Summer Movie Series** at the **Ohio Theatre**. For less than $10, you and your date can both get tickets to the classics. We suggest taking a seat in the balcony, where you can watch movies such as *Roman Holiday*, *North by Northwest* and even a few modern-day classics such as *Raiders of the Lost Ark*. Save even more by buying a strip of 10 tickets. *39 E. State St., Columbus, 614-469-1045, www.capa.com.*

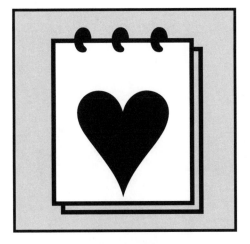

DATE
CALENDAR

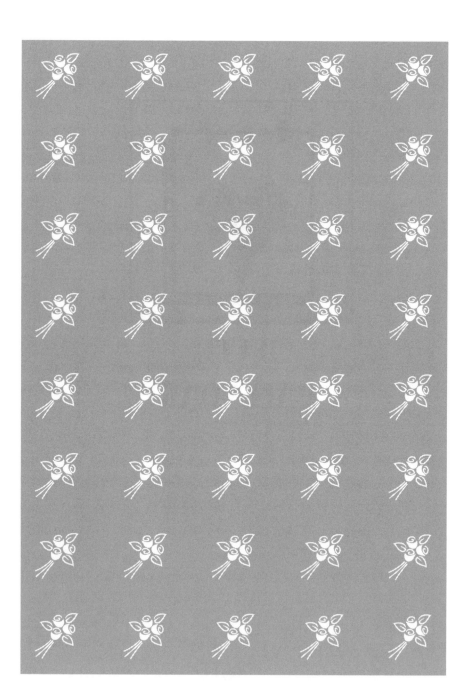

The following is a short listing of annual romantic and date-worthy Columbus-area events. Some happenings run for more than one month, especially summer activities. Many of the events work as a couples-only date, or as family dates. For more ideas on events, exhibitions, concerts and other activities, visit the Experience Columbus Web site at www.experiencecolumbus.com.

January

Columbus Bride: The Show. For couples ready to make the plunge, more than 160 vendors are on hand to hawk their wares from wedding cakes to flower girl dresses. Fashion shows daily during weekend event usually held at Veterans Memorial. *300 W. Broad St., Columbus, 614-540-5900, www.columbusbride.com/theshow.html.*

Shadowbox Cabaret: Sex at the 'Box. Shadowbox Cabaret presents its annual Sex at the 'Box revue with sexy, humorous skits, along with its famous in-house rock cover band, BillWho?. Runs January through March. *164 Easton Town Center, Columbus, 614-416-7625, www.shadowboxcabaret.com.*

February

In Love with BalletMet. Catch one of BalletMet's February performances, which usually include productions full of passion and star-crossed lovers. Past performances have included *A Midsummer Night's Dream* and a recent production centering on Ravel's *Bolero*. *614-229-4860, www.balletmet.org.*

Sweethearts Hike. Take an evening stroll with your loved one to Ash Cave, the largest recess cave in Ohio. Warm up with a campfire and refreshments afterward. *Off St. Rte. 56, Logan, 740-385-6842 or 800-HOCKING, www.1800hocking.com.*

March

Blooms & Butterflies. The swallowtails and icy blue morphs return to the Franklin Park Conservatory each spring for a beautiful butterfly spectacular inside the conservatory. Butterflies are on release through the beginning of September. *1777 E. Broad St., Columbus, 614-645-TREE, www.fpconservatory.org.*

April

Baseball Season Begins. Take your date out to the ball game as the Columbus Clippers start their season of minor-league, AAA baseball. Make it a Cheap Date during dime-a-dog games. Season runs through the beginning of September. *1155 W. Mound St., Columbus, 614-462-5250, www.clippersbaseball.com.*

Earth Day. Make your own Earth Day celebration on April 23 with a tree planting or trip together to the recycling center. The Columbus Zoo and Aquarium is one of the few central Ohio locations that sponsors an annual celebration with exhibits and activities. *9990 Riverside Dr., Powell, 614-645-3550, www.colszoo.org.*

May

Concerts on the Village Green. Worthington's live summer concert series starts its season, which runs through August. Performances take place Sunday evenings on the historic downtown green. *Corner of N. High Street and St. Rte. 161, 614-436-2743, www.worthington.org.*

Village Valuables & Bier Garten. German Village plays host to the city's largest yard sale with more than 100 sellers. It's a treasure-trove for those just setting up house. For shopping fortification, brew and brats are available at the German Village Meeting Haus. *588 S. Third St., Columbus, 614-221-8888, www.germanvillage.com.*

PGA Memorial Golf Tournament. One of the area's most famous annual events, the Memorial brings out the big-time players from founder Jack Nicklaus to phenom Tiger Woods. Bring an umbrella built for two to this typically rainy event, which starts with practice rounds during Memorial Day weekend. *5750 Memorial Dr., Dublin, 614-889-6700, www.thememorialtournament.com.*

June

Columbus Arts Festival. For more than 40 years, this has been Columbus' premier arts event. More than 300 artists and crafters assemble on the east side of the Scioto River to sell everything from jewelry to sculpture. *Downtown riverfront, 614-224-2606, www.gcac.org.*

Festival Latino. Ohio's largest celebration of Hispanic/Latino culture. This multi-day festival features music, dance, food, art and a marketplace. *Bicentennial and Genoa Parks, Downtown, 614-645-3800, www.festivallatino.net.*

Literary Picnics. Join acclaimed authors for an evening of picnicking, readings, Q&A, and book signings at the Thurber House. Guests can bring their own picnic or buy a dinner ticket. Picnics run through August, including a family picnic. *77 Jefferson Ave., Columbus, 614-464-1032, www.thurberhouse.org.*

Shakespeare in the Park. Actors' Theatre starts its annual season of free Shakespeare in the Park performances at Schiller Park in German Village. Bring a blanket and a picnic to this free event, with performances through Labor Day weekend. *1000 City Park Ave., Columbus, 614-444-6888, www.theactorstheatre.org.*

CAPA Summer Movie Series. Watch classic movies such as *To Kill a Mockingbird* or *To Catch a Thief* in the gorgeous surroundings of the Ohio Theatre. Pre- and post-show and intermission entertainment with music from the Mighty Morton Theatre Organ add to the experience. Runs through August. *39 E. State St., 614-469-1045, www.capa.com.*

Short North Sunday Jazz Series. Listen to favorite local jazz artists perform on the gazebo stage at Goodale Park with a pretty pond backdrop. Season typically runs from June through August. Concerts begin at noon and are free. *120 W. Goodale Blvd., 614-645-3800, www.musicintheair.org/snsjazz.html.*

German Village Haus und Garten Tour. Tour some of the area's finest historical homes together for a little inspiration. Gardening demonstrations and a watercolor competition also take place. Sponsored by the German Village Society. *588 S. Third St., Columbus, 614-221-8888, www.germanvillage.com.*

July

Red, White & Boom. We don't necessarily recommend going to the overcrowded downtown event—one of the largest fireworks displays in the Midwest—but there are plenty of out-of-the-way places to watch the show that won't leave you gasping for space, such as the west campus parking lots at Ohio State University or the observation deck at Chestnut Ridge Metro Park. *614-421-BOOM, www.redwhiteandboom.org.*

Picnic with the Pops. Enjoy an outdoor picnic while listening to the Columbus Symphony Orchestra perform classics and pop tunes accompanied by various artists, including the Ohio State University Marching Band (you can even get catered tailgate food) during the season finale in August. *Lawn of Chemical Abstracts, 2540 Olentangy River Rd., Columbus, 614-228-8600, www.picnicwiththepops.com.*

Topiary Garden Concerts. On Tuesdays from July through August, you can spend a pleasant lunch hour listening to performances in the Topiary Garden, the come-to-life topiary depiction of Georges Seurat's famous painting *A Sunday Afternoon on the Island of La Grand Jatte.* Lunches may also be available for purchase in the park. Concerts start at 11:30 a.m. *E. Town St. and Washington Ave. (behind the Columbus Main library), 614-645-3800, www.musicintheair.org/tgconcerts.html.*

August

Ohio State Fair. The animals, the extra-thick milkshakes from the dairy producers, and a huge midway area are just a few of the highlights during this 12-day event. Snuggle up together for a Sky Ride tour of the action below. *717 E. 17th Ave., 888-OHO-EXPO, www.ohioexpocenter.com/osf/osf.htm.*

September

Greek Festival. Each Labor Day weekend the Greek Orthodox Cathedral in the Short North Arts District opens its doors for cathedral tours and festival fun. Music, dancing, Greek food and pastries highlight the celebration. *555 N. High St., Columbus, 614-224-9020, www.greekcathedral.com.*

Upper Arlington Labor Day Arts Festival. End summer with another Labor Day tradition, the UA Arts Festival at Northam Park, filled with entertainment, family activities, and art for purchase. *2070 Northam Rd., Upper Arlington, 614-583-5310, www.ua-ohio.net/artsfestival.*

German Village Oktoberfest. Usually in September or October, the Oktoberfest is a celebration of German culture, food and beer. Live entertainment and plenty of kegs keep the fun coming. *Corner of South Grant & E. Livingston Avenues, 614-221-8888, www.germanvillage.com.*

October

Halloween Ghost Walks. Keep close together as the Columbus Landmarks Foundation leads ghost-seekers on a tour of the city's most haunted sites. *61 Jefferson Ave., Columbus, 614-221-0227, www.columbuslandmarks.org.*

Hayrides & Harvest Moonlight Tours. Each Saturday in October, Malabar Farm State Park treats guests to hayrides, hot cider and a camp fire on the grounds where one of Hollywood's most romantic couples, Lauren Bacall and Humphrey Bogart, was married. *4050 Bromfield Rd., Lucas, 419-892-2784, www.malabarfarm.org.*

November
Wildlights. Millions of lights cast a glow on the Columbus Zoo and Aquarium beginning around Thanksgiving. Annual offerings include an ice rink, horse-drawn wagon rides, hot cocoa and roasted nuts. Runs through the beginning of January. *9990 Riverside Dr., Powell, 614-645-3550, www.colszoo.org.*

December
The Nutcracker. BalletMet's annual interpretation of the Tchaikovsky classic comes alive in the Ohio Theatre, including performances by the Columbus Symphony Orchestra and the Columbus Children's Choir. *39 E. State St., 614-229-4860, www.balletmet.org.*

First Night Columbus. This annual event kicks off the new year and ends the old with concerts, live entertainment, family activities and fire-works in several downtown locations from 4:30 p.m. Dec. 31st until after midnight Jan. 1. *Downtown Columbus, 614-481-0020, www.firstnightcolumbus.com.*

Romantic
GIFT
Finder

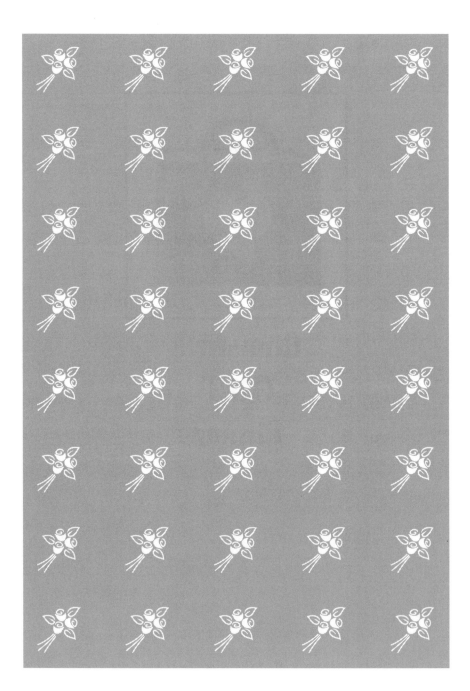

Gift giving in relationships is often fraught with tension and questions. One big reason: gifts are seen as barometers for the relationship. Do you understand me? Are you paying attention? What if my gift doesn't meet his or her expectations? At what point in a relationship is it appropriate to give a gift? Should there be a spending limit based on the length of the relationship? What do you give your love after years in a relationship?

The best advice: Go with your heart. And if you need a little help expressing your gift of love, use some of the ideas in this chapter to inspire you.

Artistic Accessories

Diamonds are a girl's best friend, but usually the gift occasion requires something a little less dazzling (and less expensive). Even so, jewelry almost always makes a great romantic gift and there are several unique options to be found at the **ARTcetera** gift shop at the Columbus Cultural Arts Center, handcrafted by the center's students. Proceeds benefit the students and the center. *139 W. Main St., Columbus, 614-645-7047, www.culturalartscenteronline.org.* Or try the gift shop at the **Columbus Museum of Art** for unique baubles. *480 E. Broad St., 614-221-6801, www.columbusmuseum.org.*

Handcrafted jewelry, along with handmade silk scarves, perfume bottles, ceramic vases and even well-crafted note cards also can be found at the **Ohio Craft Museum** gift shop. From mid-November through just before Christmas the museum converts into one big sale exhibit known as the Gifts of the Craftsmen. Closed Saturdays, except during Gifts of the Craftsmen. *1665 W. Fifth Ave., Columbus, 614-486-4402, www.ohiocraft.org/museum.html.*

Royal Scentsation

Want to surprise your date with a unique scent or one worn by royalty? **Luxe de vie** in the Short North is the only place in town that stocks "Bond No. 9" (a line of perfumes from New York, $150-$200) and "Human" by Fruits & Passions. They also carry perfume by one of the oldest perfume makers in the world, The House of Creed, from Paris, also known as the royal perfumers of Europe. You can even purchase the same scent Prince Rainier had made as a wedding gift for his bride-to-be Grace Kelly ("Sleurissimo"). Want your man to wear a royal scent? Try "Irish Tweed," which is a favorite of Prince Charles. *720 N. High St., Columbus, 614-421-0589, www.luxedevie.com.*

Wrapped Up in Red

When the packaging is almost as good as the gift—or nothing says "I love you" like a big red box—order a gift for your loved one from **Red Envelope**. The online retailer has taken a page from Tiffany's. Deliveries from the gift company arrive in classic red boxes tied with cream-colored ribbons. Shop for everything from romantic gifts for her (silk boxers for ladies) to romantic gifts for him (kama sutra weekender kit, which includes pleasure balm, sweet almond massage oil and honey dust with a feather applicator). The site also features a selection of anniversary gifts by year, for when you just don't know if it's the year of paper or linen. *877-733-3683, www.redenvelope.com.*

Basket Bounty

You might not know the name, but more than likely you've noticed the storefront for **Baskets by Bonnie** on the corner of Buttles and High streets in the Short North. The store stocks all sorts of creative items, including pink flamingos to put in the yard of your lovebird. You can shop with a supermarket-type basket or allow Bonnie and her staff to guide you. Customers can choose from specialty themed baskets, such as the Italian Mini Hamper, which includes everything for an Italian dinner at home, or you can have a basket custom-made specifically with your sweetheart in mind. Baskets can be shipped nationwide or hand delivered to several area neighborhoods. *721 N. High St., Columbus, 614-228-8700, www.basketsbybonnie.com.*

Cuddle Bears

No need to wait for the Ohio State Fair to give your loved one a teddy bear. At **Build-A-Bear Workshop** at Easton or Tuttle Crossing, you pick the type of stuffed animal (bear, horse, cat or other lovable) and add the details. Perhaps a frog that ribbets or a monkey that makes real monkey sounds? You can also record different sayings so your sweetie can hear you say "I love you" with just a squeeze. People have even recorded marriage proposals and had diamond rings sewn onto their cuddly creations. Add a heart, blow in a few of your kisses and watch as the critter is stuffed while you wait. It will make you remember young love all over again. *3995 Gramercy St., Columbus, 614-473-8888 or 5043 Tuttle Crossing Blvd., Dublin, 614-336-8319, www.buildabear.com.*

Handmade from the Heart

Make your own artistic statement of love at places such as the **Clay Cafe Co.** in Grandview, where you can create your own hand-painted coffee mug or teapot or coaster. You don't have to be an artist to do it. Think of all the grade-school art projects treasured over the years. When you're done with your Picasso, pick it up a few days later, and then proudly wrap it up for your loved one. *1431 W. Third Ave., Columbus, 614-486-5815.*

At the **Woodcraft** store in Hilliard you can sign up for classes such as building bookcases, creating 18th-century-style furniture or making bottle stoppers (just be sure to add the velvet-wrapped bottle of wine to go with it). *4562 Cemetery Rd., Hilliard, 614-527-7594, www.woodcraft.com.* (For any of these ideas, just be sure to plan extra time.)

Art for Our Sake

If making your own gift is intimidating, then stroll through the galleries in the **Short North Arts District**. You'll find everything from pottery to paintings to glasswork and more made by local and national artists. Start at Goodale and High St. and work your way north and south, *www.shortnorth.org.*

Each December **Columbus College of Art and Design** holds a one-day sale of student artwork. You're sure to find interesting jewelry, photography, sculptures, glasswork, paintings and more, plus you'll be helping future professional artists pay for their tuition to one of the best art schools in the country (and no black velvet in sight). *107 N. Ninth St., Columbus, 614-224-9101, www.ccad.edu.*

Naughty Niceties

Columbus has its own test market for lingerie—the **Victoria's Secret North** store at Easton. It's one of the advantages of having a major retail empire based in Columbus. At the Vickie's across from Smith & Wollensky, you'll find lacy and racy things here first before they reach the rest of the country. They carry everything from the Pink cotton collection of sleepwear to the Sexy Little Things line of skimpy pink and black evening wear in the 8,000-square-foot display space. The store even has a selection of cosmetics sure to make you pucker up. *4115 The Strand West, Columbus, 614-476-5877, www.victoriassecret.com.*

The Finishing Touch

Places such as **Peabody's Papers** in Grandview provide the perfect finishing touch for gifts. You'll find things such as wrapping paper made from Paris and London street maps, scented drawer liners and stationery perfect for writing your love note. They are also a great place to get unique invitations for that special party. *1261 Grandview Ave., Columbus, 614-485-9855.*

For unique floral arrangements try **Steven Cox Flowers**, located in the restored Hartman Building downtown. They buy off the Dutch market, so anytime of year you can select everything from French tulips to hydrangeas to orange winterberry, red amaryllis and more. *265 S. Fourth St., Columbus, 614-224-6555.* Depending upon the season, you can also find armfuls of sunflowers, lilies, orchids and more at the **Market Blooms** floral shop in the middle of the North Market, *614-228-7760.* While you're there stop by the **Grapes of Mirth** and pick from the local merchant's well-stocked wine collection, *614-221-9463. North Market, 59 Spruce St., Columbus, www.northmarket.com.*

Site and Organization Index

About the
AUTHORS

Amber Stephens is a freelance
writer and editor whose work has appeared in
several local and regional publications. She
writes from her historic home in rural Amanda
where she is a stay-at-home mom to her two
young children, Samuel and Amelia. When she
isn't running the "farm" and taking care of the
kids, she enjoys going on great date research
outings with her husband, Bill.

Jennifer Poleon is a poet, artist, veteran travel writer and
editor and co-founder of Emuses Press. Over the
course of her decade-plus career, she has served
as an editor for *Ohio* and *Columbus Parent* magazines, winning many writing awards for her
work, including a nod from the Ohio Society of
Professional Journalists for Best Public
Journalism for a story she did on the Columbus
Public Schools. Poleon is currently the Director
of Communications for the Ohio Travel
Association and an adjunct professor at
Columbus State Community College, where she
co-founded the college's student newspaper, *CougarNews*. Her travels
have taken her to the streets of Prague, the back roads of Italy, the coast
of Maine, the canyons and red cliffs of New Mexico, and of course,
many romantic and out-of-the-way places in Ohio.

About the
PUBLISHER

Emuses was founded in December 2000 by former *Ohio Magazine* staffers Jennifer Poleon, Robin Smith and Kathy Murphy to offer publication design and editorial services to clients in central Ohio and beyond. In 2002 Emuses published *Columbus Ghosts: Historic Haunts of Ohio's Capital* by Robin Smith, then *Columbus Ghosts II: More Central Ohio Haunts,* also by Smith, in 2003. With *Kissing in Columbus*, we address another aspect of life in central Ohio and enter the mainstream of travel guide publishing. Planned future books will further explore the many faces of the Buckeye state.

We'd love to hear from you about our books. Write us at
Emuses
P.O. Box 1264
Worthington, OH 43085-1264

Or e-mail us at
info@emusespress.com

Visit our Web site at www.emusespress.com

Have an idea for a book?

While we are truly a small press and plan to publish a limited number of titles per year, your proposal may be the magic one! Send us a *short* written outline of your proposed book (no more than two pages, please) with a sample chapter for our review. Please remember to include complete contact information: name, address, phone, and e-mail and a short author biography.

We cannot return submitted materials. Do not include any original art or send your only copy of your manuscript.

Enjoy KISSING in COLUMBUS?

Order copies for friends and check out our other Emuses titles!

Columbus Ghosts: Historical Haunts of Ohio's Capital
Thoroughly researched and beautifully written by Robin Smith, *Columbus Ghosts* uncovers both Columbus' past and the spirits of those who lived it. Scorned women, a most eccentric pharmacist, a President and his jealous wife, grieving parents, and soldier boys in blue and gray—all these and more live on in *Columbus Ghosts*. It's Columbus history with a twist!

Columbus Ghosts II: More Central Ohio Haunts
And you thought the haunts of Columbus were all distant historical specters? Think again, as Robin Smith reveals not only more historical shades, but some of the contemporary spirits inhabiting the homes, theaters and public places of Columbus and central Ohio. Heroes and villains, professors and prostitutes, fathers and firefighters–meet 'em and shiver.

Just send this form with a check or money order (payable to Emuses) to Emuses, P.O. Box 1264, Worthington, OH 43085

Title	Quantity	Price per book	Total
Kissing in Columbus		$16.95	
Columbus Ghosts		$13.95	
Columbus Ghosts II		$13.95	
For more than three books or to order books for resale, e-mail info@emusespress.com	Ohio residents add appropriate sales tax for your county		
	Shipping/handling add $4.50 (for up to three books)		
	TOTAL ENCLOSED		

Name

Address

City/State/ZIP

Phone   E-mail address